# A STANDARD FOR MILLER

## A Community Response to Pornography

Edward J. Shaughnessy
Diana Trebbi

UNIVERSITY
PRESS OF
AMERICA

82-4350

## ACKNOWLEDGEMENTS

The Clinton-Times Square Survey was conducted under a grant from the Chas. E. Culpeper Foundation, U.N. Plaza, New York City.

CONTENTS

LIST OF TABLES

## Preface

During the past few years, the adult entertainment industry has taken a highly visible form
in New York City's entertainment center, Times
Square. The visible presence of the industry is
defined by street level massage parlors, peepshows,
"x-rated" movie houses, bookstores and shops
purveying adult materials, live sex shows, and
topless and bottomless bars. In carrying on its
trade, the sex industry has impinged upon a tradi-
tionally residential neighborhood adjacent to Times
Square called Clinton. Explicit depiction of
sexual activities in street advertisements of
x-rated movies and photographs fronting massage
parlors have created concern in the Clinton community. On the behavioral side and equally a matter claiming the consideration of Clinton residents
are aggressive soliciting tactics of street prostitutes and persons distributing advertising
leaflets for massage parlors, fronts for prostitution.

This community concern has been expressed by
area residents to the researchers. In a mini-
survey conducted in January 1977, community residents were approached on the question of the impact of adult entertainment on the area. These
residents were also leaders in contact with large
numbers of Clinton people; i.e., the chairman of
Community Board 4, principals of Clinton schools
and their PTA heads, local church and political
leaders. When asked to rank sex-related activities in a numbered list of seven community problems, 10 out of 12 leaders asked ranked adult
uses in first or second place.

It was the recognition of the concern for the
well being of the community expressed by its residents and leaders that prompted the authors to
undertake this study. )The confusion over the

determination of a community standard as articulated by <u>Miller v California</u> (1973) made the need for this study imperative.

Judges have frequently placed the burden of determination of what constitutes a community standard in the hands of a trial jury. Such "ad hoc" random determinations are productive of inconsistency in trial outcomes and a lack of even handedness in setting up regulations for the acceptable display of materials and permissible activities. The end result has been the growth of the adult entertainment industry.

A model study of a community which can be replicated elsewhere will enable responsible residents and leaders to come to defensible determinations of a community standard of obscenity/pornography which can be measured objectively and viewed coherently beyond the preference of a petit jury and consistent with the parameters of free speech.

A special word of thanks are due to Mary D'Elia, co-leader of the Clinton District for the Democratic Party, and Ms. Helen Dolan, survey office manager. The project data was prepared and analyzed expertly by Professor William Burger of the Sociology Department at John Jay College of Criminal Justice.

The publication of a statistical manuscript
is a complicated and demanding process. It
requires graphic skills, patient scaling and care-
ful layouts for tables. The fine quality of
Technical work in this book is due to the uncom-
promising effort and generous labors of Peter
Dodenhoff, Editor of Law Enforcement News and
Laura Kelly, Production Manager. Marie Rosen,
Operations Manager of the Office of Publications,
patiently oversaw the collaboration of all the
components of this monograph. I am grateful to
the personnel of these offices for their unfialing
courtesy and cooperative spirit in the face of this
major intrusion into their already hectic schedules.

Finally, a special word of deep appreciation
is expressed to Mrs. Elizabeth Cruz for her
typing of the manuscript through revisions,
corrections and tabular modification. She worked
with professional skill, unfailing patience and
boundless good will. The photography was done
by Wagner Photoprint. The index was prepared by
Dolores Grande.

CHAPTER I

STATEMENT OF THE PROBLEM

I. STATEMENT OF THE PROBLEM

For the first time since its 1957 Roth
decision, a majority of the Supreme Court agreed
upon concrete guidelines for separating obscenity
from constitutionally protected speech in the
Miller case in 1973.(1) This landmark decision
specified criteria to be used in determining
whether or not material was legally obscene.(2)
As stated in Miller, the history of the Supreme
Court's obscenity decisions is somewhat "tex-
tured": apart from the initial formulation in
Roth(3) and the reformulation in Miller, no
majority of the court has at any given time been
able to agree on a standard to determine what
constitutes obscene, pornographic matter, subject
to regulation under the state's police power;
instead there was

> a variety of views among the members
> of the court unmatched in any other
> course of constitutional adjudication.

The court went on to say that

> this uncertainty of the standards for
> dealing with obscenity creates a con-
> tinuing source of tension between state
> and federal courts; ~~that~~ the problem is
> that one cannot say with certainty that
> material is obscene until at least five
> members of the court, applying obscure
> standards, have pronounced it so.(4)

The ensuing confusion with regard to interpretation of the Miller decision has caused difficulty
to the criminal justice system in enforcing
extant statutes relating to the pornographic

entertainment business. Hence, there has developed a type of sex business, which is stubbornly resistant to permanent closing particularly in downtown urban areas. The Supreme Court's attempt in _Miller_ to sharply delineate criteria under which a work could be considered obscene operates today under such concepts as "legal offensiveness" and psycho-legal explanations of the term "prurient interest."(5)

Despite repeated assertions in _Roth_, _Miller_, and _Paris Adult Theatre I_ that obscene material is not speech entitled to First Amendment protection, it is a fact that obscenity is no longer an exception to freedom of speech and the press in the traditional meaning of those terms. However, even the liberal justices of the present Supreme Court, the dissenters from the Burger view, have allowed that expression can in certain ways be restricted. That is, the citizen who has something he wishes to communicate may not be silenced completely - he can be as obscene about it as he likes - but the flow of his expression can be channeled. These liberal justices have said that the First Amendment is not infringed by anti-obscenity laws that seek to safeguard children or to prevent the infliction of unwanted displays on a captive audience.

Legitimate problems with the protection of free speech remain, then, regarding the protection of children, the unwilling audience, and especially in the matter of prostitution: behavior mixed with expression.(6) In the case of _Young v. The American Mini-Theatre Inc._, the Supreme Court, by a 5-4 decision on June 24, 1976, held that a city had the right to regulate and control property uses for the purpose of adult entertainment as a separate and distinct use. The court further held

3

that such cases could be prohibited from areas adjacent to residential neighborhoods and that the city of Detroit had shown a compelling state interest sufficient to validate the restrictions imposed upon otherwise protected speech activities. Justice Stevens, in writing for the majority of the court, employed the arguments for his decision: "...the city's interest in attempting to preserve the quality of urban life," and "concern for the present and future character of its neighborhoods."(7)

The past five years have seen civil libertarians put forth vigorous efforts to prevent governmental interference with First Amendment protection of speech and the press in the matter of obscenity. Harriet Pilpel of the American Civil Liberties Union(8) has stated that the Union's only concession on the question of obscenity cases is the concept of the "unwilling audience", which aspect she sees as actionable under the law.

The National Coalition Against Censorship sees the recent Smith decision of the Supreme Court as further eroding First Amendment freedoms under the community standards doctrine enunciated in Miller.(9)  In this case Smith, indicted on May 23, 1977(10) in southern Iowa for mailing obscene materials in violation of the 1873 Comstock Act, attempted to question jurors about their knowledge of contemporary southern Iowa standards on obscenity.  The Court opinion held: (1) state law cannot define contemporary community standards for appeal to prurient interest and patent offensiveness that apply under Miller in determining whether material is obscene; therefore, any Iowa obscenity statute is inconclusive as to those standards.  Those issues are in fact questions for the jury, to be judged in light of

Smith

4

of its understanding of contemporary community standards. (2) State legislatures cannot declare what community standards shall be, any more than they could undertake to define "reasonableness."(11) (3) The Comstock Act of 1873 was enacted under Congress' constitutional postal power, not its commerce power. A state's right not to regulate in the obscenity field cannot correlatively compel the Federal Government to allow the mails to be used to send obscene materials into that state.

In fact, some of the Supreme Court Justices themselves have shown concern for infringement of First Amendment freedoms in dissenting from the majority view in certain obscenity cases. In his minority opinion in the case of <u>Smith,</u> J. Stevens states:

> The critical First Amendment question in this kind of case involves the interested individual's right of access to materials he desires.(12)

And further:

> The conclusion that a uniformly administered national standard is incapable of definition or administration is a reason for questioning the suitability of criminal prosecution as the mechanism for regulating the distribution of erotic material.(13)

J. Brennan, in dissenting from the decision in <u>Paris Adult Theatre I v. Slaton,</u> used the same reasoning he had employed in another court decision on obscenity:

It is contended that the State's
action was justified because the motion
picture attractively portrays a relationship which is contrary to the moral
standards, religious precepts, and legal
code of its citizenry.  This argument mis-
conceives what it is that the Constitution protects.  Its guarantee is not
confined to the expression of ideas that
are conventional or shared by a majority.
It protects advocacy of the opinion
that adultery may sometimes be proper, no
less than the advocacy of socialism or
the single tax.  And in the realm of
ideas, it protects expression which is
eloquent no less than that which is
unconvincing.(14)

The growth of activities of a possibly obscene nature, yet to be defined by any community
standard, has increasingly involved the display
of materials advertising such activities.  This
poses significant questions at the street level
for law enforcement and legislative officials.
Various attempts to develop or define a community
standard on obscenity have not met with success,
and as a matter of fact, the 1977 Smith decision
discussed above, would seem to create a "chilling"
effect on attempts to develop local, regional or
statewide standards of obscenity.(15)

Discouraged by the uncertainty surrounding
the recent history of obscenity decisions, some
cities in the past year have attempted to deal
with the conflicting rights involved when pornography attempts to exist side by side with
neighborhood life by turning to the zoning solution, taken by the city of Detroit as a result of
the Young decision.  In January, 1977, the New

York City Planning Commission published proposed
amendments to the zoning resolution section of
the City Charter.(16)   As an enforcement tool,
the New York proposal differentiates between two
kinds of land uses:  x-rated (adult use) and others.

Of late, attempts to regulate adult entertainment activities have involved actions against
individual establishments under the civil law,
particularly the sections on public and private
nuisances.  The law literature on alternative approaches to the problem of obscenity, mainly
published since 1975 in the State of California,
points to considering obscenity as a public or
private nuisance and applying civil remedies for
that nuisance.(17)   To constitute a public nuisance in California, conduct must fall within a
range of its Civil Code.  The public nuisance must
be either:  1) injurious to health, when a great
number of people are drawn into a small area,
thereby creating traffic and fire hazards.  When
the presence of adult entertainment establishments
creates a new sexual permissiveness among community members, it may increase the occurrence of
unwanted pregnancies and venereal disease.  Proof
of this is not needed:  it may be enough that            .
the community's fears on these eventualities are
real.  2) an obstruction to the free use of property.  A community may try to demonstrate that
the presence of adult entertainment in its midst
caused the value of the property within the
neighborhood of the establishment to diminish.
It can be shown that congregations of loiterers
attracted by sex businesses interfere with everyday comings and goings of neighboring homeowners
or tenants, and statutory requirements will be
satisfied.  3) conduct indecent and offensive to
the senses.

The real key to the satisfaction of the
nuisance definition in pornography cases is to

show that the conduct complained of is indecent or offensive to the senses. Most nuisances are so to the perceptory senses, but California has a long case history of conduct offensive to the moral senses, which can also be a public nuisance. Sex businesses must affect the entire neighborhood to be considered a public nuisance. The character of the community wherein the alleged public nuisance is located would play a major role in determining the existence of injury. Where sex businesses deal continually with pornographic materials, a community may show an increase in crime or criminal elements in and around the immediate area of the establishments. To provide for First Amendment protection for some materials, it must be shown also that the material is obscene. The concept of a private nuisance has to do with an individual's right to privacy. To argue that sex businesses constitute a private nuisance in California, it must be shown that: 1) there is unreasonable interference with the right to enjoy a residence; 2) that this interference is also substantial; i.e., that reasonable precautions have been taken to this end by the resident and that there exist some degree of permanence in the interference. In presenting the pornography problem as either a public or a private nuisance to the community involved, the court would probably be most sympathetic to a parent's concern that children may be exposed to offensive displays in the course of normal domestic activity.

In New York's Civil Law Code, there is a quite detailed section defining a nuisance and prescribing steps toward its abatement.(18)  The State Law declares that public nuisances as known at common law are unlawful.(19)  In another attempt to deal with spreading Times Square pornography, a New York City Local Law was passed by the City

Council on June 21, 1977. Known as the Nuisance
Abatement Law(20) it is based on civil rather than
criminal law. Taking immediate effect, it amended
the administrative code fo the city in defining
certain illegal sex oriented businesses as nuisances. The statute empowers the New York City Corporation counsel to maintain civil actions on behalf
of the City against any of the nuisance defined
in the statute. But it seems, especially in its
definition of public nuisances in Secs. b) and c)
of the Amendment, which deal with "obscene" performances and the promotion of "obscene" material,
that once again, New York City is attempting to
set up a local standard of the concept of obscenity
set down by our Supreme Court in the Miller case.
This as has already been demonstrated is only applicable on a case by case basis, and when applied,
arouses controversy among the U. S. Supreme Court
Justices themselves.

Rendelman sees the law, at least at the state
legislative level, moving slowly but inexorably
toward less instrusive methods of regulating
obscenity.(21)  He advocates that states abandon
criminal penalties in favor of an exclusive civil
remedy providing for injunctive relief against
obscenity.  Rendelman's view sees equity procedures
according a civilized warning to businesses, reducing
the stigma of state control of sex entertainments,
and focusing on the critical issue of obscenity rather
than on irrelevant procedures.

The 18-step statute advocated by Rendelman as
a specific civil reguoltory instrument for obscenity
suggests, as the first step, that courts of general
jurisdiction shall judge whether the...matter is
obscene.  Here again, it seems that a determination
of obscenity will have to base itself on the Miller
criteria.

## II. OTHER RELEVANT RESEARCH

The experience of the following researchers in attempting to quantify and standardize reactions to potentially obscene material, would seem to confirm the fact that in the last analysis, the judgmental processes involved in labeling material "obscene" are indeed very volatile. Personal perceptions of obscenity also vary greatly with each individual(22) and are subject to the distortion of social influences. D. H. Wallace, in a survey of adults from the Detroit metropolitan area, sought the elucidation of a "community standard" on obscenity. He concluded that there is no single standard used by the respondents in their evaluation of a series of erotic pictures.(23) The study points to a major difficulty in determining a fixed community attitude on obscenity.

In a study of the effects of attitude and perceived physiological reaction in evaluating pornographic films, Colson found that low subject tolerance to erotica, pedophilia and GSR(24) feedback indicated the passages labeled as more obscene and unfavorable. Medical students in the group who had been told that GSR feedback meant sexual arousal gave more favorable ratings to the film passages shown.(25)

A different analytical approach to pornography is found in Kirkpatrick's recent researches on collective behavior and anti-pornography crusades. Kirkpatrick develops a collective behavior theory from Durkheim's The Division of Labor in Society which predicts the severity of a collective outburst according to the degree to which the crime (pornography) is publicly designated a flagrant threat to the collective consciousness. Part of Kirkpatrick's theory is the fact that it is not the deviance itself but rather the style of the deviant;

10

i.e., public visibility and probability of success
in his enterprise, which determines the severity
of the community reaction.

Kirkpatrick compared community attempts to
abate pornographic activities in two American
cities which he named Southtown and Midville.
In Southtown, there were fewer newspaper reports
of ongoing pornographic businesses, smaller
attendance at anti-pornographic rallies, and
fewer signers of a petition to ban pornography
than in Midville. In Southtown, owner-operators
of sex businesses cooperated in self-censorship,
while those in Midville refused to cooperate
with the authorities, and filed suit against the
city and the organization pursuing them; charging
that their constitutional rights had been violated.
In Midville, speeches against pornographers on
the part of various governmental officials, law
enforcement officers, leading citizens, and candidates for public office, coalesced the community
attitude toward the nuisance. Kirkpatrick con-
cludes that a high public visibility, the probability of success on the part of the pornographers,
and public designation of the deviance by "prestige"
figures contributed to a much more intense anti-
pornography movement in Midville.(26)

As part of the empirical research funded by
the Commission on Obscenity and Pornography,
Kirkpatrick collaborated with R. A. Zurcher to
expand this project into a book whose thesis is
that anti-pornography crusades are conservative
symbolic crusades.(27) They based this idea on
the findings of Gusfield's 1963 study(28) of the
American temperance movement. Gusfield concluded
that the temperance crusade, as a social movement,

11

was a way by which members of a status group could strive to preserve, defend, or enhance the prestige of their style of life against threats from individuals or groups whose lifestyle differed from theirs. Zurcher and Kirkpatrick hypothesized that (following Gusfield) anti-pornography crusades would manifest status politics, escalated to the level of symbolic crusades by the concerted activities of status discontents. These are individuals who perceived as threatened the prestige and attendant power of the lifestyle to which they were committed. Kirkpatrick and Zurcher saw the anti-pornography efforts of women's liberation groups as liberal symbolic crusades. Both conservative and liberal symbolic crusades are the status political acts of individuals who are status discontents attempting to enhance the prestige and power of their lifestyles.

Smelser(29) argues that "antiporns" will cite their commitment to and concern over "basic" societal values and will act collectively to restore, protect, modify, or create norms in the name of a generalized belief. They will call for new laws and regulatory devices concerning pornography which are intended to control the "irresponsible" behavior of others, who will be seen to be deviating from "established" patterns of behavior and thereby to be threatening "social order" and "basic values".

# FOOTNOTES

1. <u>Miller v. California</u> (1973) 413 U.S. 15; 93 ~~3~~
   Sup. CT. 2607

2. These criteria are known thereafter as the
   "Miller Test". For material to be obscene
   under this test, it must 1) appeal to prurient interest 2) violate contemporary community standards 3) be without substantial
   redeeming value in terms of political,
   scientific, social or artistic worth. The
   Court limited the class of depicted conduct
   which lawmakers may validly specify to a few
   plain examples of what obscenity statutes
   may define for regulation a) patently offensive representations or descriptions of
   ultimate sexual acts, normal or perverted,
   actual or simulated b) patently offensive
   representations or descriptions of mastur-
   bation, excretory functions, and lewd ex-
   hibitions of genitals.

3. 77 Sup. Ct. 1304 (1957)

4. As stated in a dissenting opinion by Ch.J.
   Warren joined by J. Clark, in <u>Jacobellis</u>
   <u>v. Ohio</u> (1964) 84 Sup. Ct. 1676 neither
   courts nor legislatures have been able to
   evolve a truly satisfactory definition of
   obscenity in context of the First Amendment.
   J. Harlan, dissenting opinion in the same case,
   observed that the test of obscenity within
   the Constitutional framework of guarantees of
   freedom of speech and the press, must ne-
   cessarily be "pricked out on a case-by-case
   basis." The Justice also stated that in
   the last analysis, the question of obscenity

depends on how the particular material charged happens to strike the minds of jurors or judges, and ultimately, those of a majority of the members of the U. S. Supreme Court.

5.  Former U.S. Prosecutor Larry Parrish, speaking at a forum: "Does the First Amendment Protect so-Called Obscenity?" New School For Social Research, October 17, 1977.

6.  Rembar, Charles. "Obscenity - Forget it." The Atlantic. May 1977, 37-41

7.  Official Reports of the Supreme Court, Vol. 427, U.S., Pt.1, 50-96.

8.  Speaking at forum "Does the First Amendment Protect So-Called Obscenity?" New School for Social Research, October 17, 1977.

9.  Censorship News, No. 4, 9/77.

10. Smith v. U.S. U.S. Law Week, Vol. 45, 4495-4503

11. Hamling v. U.S. 418 U.S. 87 104-105.

12. Smith v. U.S.

13. Hamling at 105.

14. Kingsley Pictures Corp. v. Regents, 360 U.S. 684, 688-689 (1959).

15. Several recent efforts come to mind. D.W. Wallace's 1973 study in Detroit is described on Page 10. In June, 1977, Mayor Ralph J. Perk and his staff of the City of Cleveland

instructed city garbage collectors to distribute 280,000 questionnaries containing 18 questions to city residents in an effort to develop a set of community standards on obscenity. The standards would be designed to meet the guidelines prescribed for juries in the Miller decision for determing what is obscene. On October 7, 1977, Mayor Frank L. Rizzo of Philadelphia signed a city ordianance that he says will rid the city of adult bookstores and pornographic movie houses. It prohibits the display or advertisement of movies, plays, books or magazines that show uncovered sexual organs; simulated or actual sexual acts, or bared female breasts unless such displays are found to have "serious literary, artistic, political, or scientific value." It also bans so-called massage parlors and prohibits display of "girlie magazines" at newsstands, drugstores and other places frequented by minors. An offense under the ordinance is punishable by up to $300 in fines and 90 days in jail. The measure is expected to be tested in the courts for its constitutionality.

16. "Amendments of the Zoning Resolution pursuant to Sec. 200 of the New York City Charter relating to various sections concerning the definition of and regulation of adult uses." City Planning Commission Calendar No. 23, Jan. 26, 1977. N 760137 ZRY.

17. "Restricting Public Display of Offensive Materials: Use and Effectiveness of Public and Private Nuisance Actions." University of San Francisco Law Review, Vol. 10:232-251 (Fall 1975)

18. N.Y. Jurisprudence. Vol. 42. Lawyers Co-
    operative Publishing Co., Rochester, N.Y.
    (1965) 443-522.

19. Penal Law of N.Y. State 1530

20. Local Law No. 55f 1977. Int. No. 1880
    6/21/77. Signed by the Council, the City
    of New York, and approved by Mayor Abraham
    D. Beame on July 28, 1977. Its legislative
    declaration reads in part:

...in the city of New York commercial ex-
ploitation of explicit sexual conduct through
the public exhibition of lewd films, the
public performance of obscene acts, the
sale of obscene publications, and the use of
so-called massage parlors and other premises for purposes of lewdness, assignation
or prostitution, constitutes a debasement
and distortion of sensitive human relation-
ships central to family life, community welfare and the development of the human person-
ality, is indecent and offensive to the senses
and to public morals and that such exploi-
tation and flagrant violations of the building
code, health laws, zoning resolutions, licensing laws, environmental laws, laws relating
to the sale and consumption of alcoholic
beverages and laws relating to gambling
and dangerous drugs all interfere with the
interest of the public in the quality
of life and total community environment,
the tone of commerce in the city, property
values and public safety; the council further finds that the continued occurrence of
such activities and violations is detrimental
to the health, safety, morals and general
welfare of the people of the city of New
York and of the businesses and visitors

thereof. It is the purpose of the council to place in one law all existing legal and equitable remedies relating to the subject matter encompassed by this law and to strengthen existing laws on the subject. This law shall apply to existing establishments which are engaged presently in the type of activities herein declared to be public nuisances in the City of New York.

The following are declared to be public nuisances:

a) Any building, erection or place used for the purpose of prostitution as defined in sec. 230.00 of the penal law. Two or more criminal convictions of persons for acts of prostitution in the building within a year preceding an action under this law shall be presumptive evidence that the building is a public nuisance. Evidence of the common fame and general reputation of the building shall be competent evidence to prove the existence of a public nuisance. Responsibility for the nuisance is imputed to owners or lessors or lessees, or anyone who maintains the public nuisance.

b) Any building used for the purposes of obscene performances. Two or more convictions for production, presentation, or direction of an obscene performance or participation in such performance within a year of the enactment of this law shall be presumptive evidence that the building is a public nuisance.

c) Any building, erection or place used for the purpose of promotion of obscene material.

17

Two or more convictions for promotion of or possession with intent to promote obscene material in the building within the one year period before the commencement of an action under this law shall be presumptive evidence that the place is a public nuisance.

d) Any building, or place used for the purpose of an business, activity or enterprise which is not licensed as required by law.

e) Any building or place wherein there is occurring a violation of the zoning resolutions of the city regulating "adult uses".

f) Any building or place where there is occurring a criminal nuisance.
See also Fordham Law Review. XLVI Oct./77 No. 1, "The Nuisance Abatement Law as a Solution to New York City's Problem of Illegal Sex-Related businesses in the Mid-Town Area." R. J. O'Connor, pp. 57-90.

21. Rendelman, D. "Civilizing Pornography: The Case for an Exclusive Obscenity Nuisance Statute". University of Chicago Law Review, Vol. 44, No. 3. Spring, 1977, 509-560.

22. See footnote 4 for J. Harlan's comment on the issue of subjectivity in judgments about obscenity.

23. Wallace, Douglas H. "Obscenity and Contemporary Community Standards: A Survey." Journal of Social Issues, 1973, 29, 3, 53-68.

24. Galvanic Skin Reflex

25. Colson, Charles E. "The Evaluation of Porno-
    graphy: Effects of Attitude and Perceived
    Physiological Reaction." Archives of Sexual
    Behavior, 1974, 3, 4, Jul. 307-323.

26. Kirkpatrick, R. George. "Collective Con-
    sciousness and Mass Hysteria: Collective
    Behavior and Anti-Pornography Crusades in
    Durkheimian Perspective." Human Relations
    (Feb. 1975) Vol. 28, 63-84.

27. Zurcher, Jr., R. A. and Kirkpatrick, R. G.
    Citizens for Decency: Antipornography Crusades
    as Status Defense. University of Texas Press,
    Austin, (1976).

28. Gusfield, J.R. Symbolic Crusade: Status Poli-
    tics and the American Temperance Movement.
    U. of Illinois Press. Urbana. (1963)

29. Smelser, N. J. Theory of Collective Behavior.
    NY Free Press (1962) p. 385.

CHAPTER II

RESEARCH METHOD AND DESIGN

# I. THE COMMUNITY

The Clinton-Times Square Survey attempted to determine whether the Clinton community adjacent to Times Square(1) could designate various activities related to pornographic entertainment as public nuisances and be willing to take steps to deal with the nuisances. This study was prompted by concern in Clinton that the spread of Times Square pornography is contributing to the deterioration of the area. The Planning Commission of New York City, pursuant to Executive Order #80 in August, 1973, designated Clinton a Neighborhood Preservation Area, with a mandate to preserve the character of its neighborhood. A portion of the Clinton(2) area was chosen for study for the following reasons:

First, Clinton is a demonstrably residential community, with solid blocks of lowrise Old Law tenements adjacent to modern luxury towers, with mixed commercial, manufacturing, and residential uses. Since the last census, numbers of Orientals have entered the area and the Hispanic population has also increased giving the area a multiethnic flavor. Of the total 1970 Census population figure, non-white population is about nine percent.

Second, the Times Square entertainment industry in general overlaps a part of this neighborhood.

Third, the Times Square adult entertainment industry as defined in this report in part overlaps the Clinton community. Hence, the exposure of Clinton residents to the adult entertainment industry is demonstrable. In developing this study, these questions came to the fore: Does the exposure have impact? If so, what kind and is it in any way

21

measurable? If there is a measurable impact, does it articulate itself in anything approximating a community consensus on the adult entertainment issue?

## II. BECOMING KNOWN IN THE WIDER COMMUNITY

Endorsements of the project were sought from Clinton leaders, as it was felt that their acquaintance with the survey would reinforce community interest. One of the researchers spoke about the survey before it was launched at Community Board No. 4 meetings and a meeting of the Clinton Planning Council. A brief announcement of the survey was entered in the local paper, CHELSEA-CLINTON NEWS and EL DIARIO, New York City's Spanish-Language daily. Just before the survey began, announcements identifying the project and those who endorsed it were sent to all the churches in the area, to be inserted into their weekly bulletin and to be read at Sunday services, by way of encouraging participation in the survey. A copy of the proposal for the survey was presented to Ms. Carol Greitzer, Councilwoman for the Times Square area.

## III. TERMS

Pornography and obscenity are defined according to Webster's Dictionary.(3) Pornography is defined as a description of prostitution, a depiction of lewdness, and a portrayal of erotic behavior designed to cause sexual excitement. Obscenity is something that is grossly repugnant to a generally accepted notion of what is appropriate; offensive, as violating some ideal or principle, or inciting to lust and depravity and having a quality of filthiness of foulness.

The adult entertainment industry comprises
five principal businesses: massage parlors,
x-rated film houses, bookstores, live sex theatres,
and coin-operated entertainment (peep shows).
It includes those who own, operate, and patronize
these businesses, and comprises prostitution.

The content of adult entertainment materials
is considered pornographic and sometimes obscene.
In order to minimize a negative judgmental approach to the questions on pornographic entertainment, all reference to pornography or obscenity in the questionnaire was replaced by use of
the term in common usage: "adult". "Adult entertainment industry" is defined as that which engages
in the manufacture, production, distribution and
exhibition or sale of "adult" viewing and reading
materials. Adult entertainment industry includes
those who own, lease, and operate premises
purveying live adult entertainment; and those who
indirectly benefit from its operations: real
estate managers and owners of companies servicing
commercial sex operations. The industry includes
prostitution.

This study defines a public nuisance as a crime
against the order and economy of the state. It
consists in unlawfully doing an act, or omit-
ting to perform a duty, which act or omission
1) annoys, injures, or endangers the comfort,
repose, health, or safety of any considerable number of persons or 2) offends public decency or 3)
unlawfully interferes with, obstructs, or renders
dangerous for passage a public park, square,
street, highway, or public waterway cleared at
public expense, or 4) in any way renders a considerable number of persons insecure in life or in
the use of property. This statute, or Penal Law
§1530, has been construed as the definition of an

offense to the public of a neighborhood or community in the enjoyment of its common rights, and not as a mere injury to a large number of persons.

In formulating a nuisance definition most applicable to the presence of adult entertainment businesses in a residential area, the study sought to answer four questions:

1) do the residents express annoyance and/or a sense of endangered health, or injury, related to the operation of these businesses?
2) is the sense of public decency offended?
3) does the operation of sex businesses unlawfully interfere with passage in streets or squares of the area?
4) does the adult entertainment industry render a considerable number of persons insecure in life or use of property?

It is important to stress that in attempting to answer the above questions, researchers hoped to determine whether or not there exists a collective sentiment on adult entertainment in Clinton. This is the part played by social science and its tools. The state's role will be to draft legislation which hopefully will take into serious account whatever sentiments are expressed by a significant number of the respondents on the issue.

There is a distinction between two types of nuisance per accidens, (in fact) and nuisance per se (matter of law). Nuisance in fact exists if the natural tendency of the act complained of is to create danger and inflict injury on person or property. Nuisance in the matter of law exists if

24

the act in its inherent nature is so hazardous
as to make the danger extreme and serious injury
so probable as to be almost a certainty. A
private nuisance is defined as is a public one
except that in the case of few people, the
special injury different from that sustained by
the general public, is at question. The same act
can constitute a public and a private nuisance.(4)

IV.  THE CLINTON-TIMES SQUARE SURVEY

Given the above legal history and sociological
setting, the researchers conducted the Clinton
study in an attempt to determine whether the
Clinton community could designate various activities related to pornographic entertainment as
public nuisances, and then exert the community
pressure which, in concert with city legislative
and enforcement agencies, will result in abating
what the community perceives to be the more offensive aspects of the adult entertainment
industry in Times Square. The "community" refer-
red to is a systematic sampling of voters registered in the five political parties of Clinton.

V.  RESEARCH METHODOLOGY

Before the survey began a mini-survey was
conducted among local Clinton leaders before
finalizing the questionnaire, to get their
assessment of the issue and to incorporate in
the questionnaire some problems and solutions
which they put forward relative to the adult
entertainment industry for possible corroboration
in the survey. Table 2.1 sets forth the result
of this effort: while narcotics was ranked as the
most serious problem six times as opposed to four
times for pornography, the pornographic trade was
mentioned a total of ten times for first or

## TABLE 2.1.

Designation of Seriousness of Pornography as a Community Problem by 12 Clinton Community Leaders - January 1977.

What do you think is the most serious problem in Clinton?

| Problem Rank | COMMUNITY LEADERS RESPONSE | | | | | | | | | | | |
|---|---|---|---|---|---|---|---|---|---|---|---|---|
|  | 1 | 2 | 3 | 4 | 5 | 6 | 7 | 8 | 9 | 10 | 11 | 12 |
| 1st | 3 |  | 5 | 6,7 | 6,7 | 2,4 |  | 5,6,7 | 7,5 | 5,7 | 7 | 4 |
| 2nd |  | 5,6,7 |  | 5 | 5 |  | 5 |  |  |  | 5 | 7,5 |
| 3rd |  |  |  |  |  |  |  |  |  |  |  |  |

Problems: 1. traffic flow; 2. lack of employment; 3. inadequate housing; 4. quality of schools; 5. pornography; 6. street crime; 7. narcotics.

second place; narcotics was designated as the number 1 or 2 problem eight times.

The study took the form of a survey questionnaire which was administered in English and Spanish by eight interviewers in a 26-square block area of Clinton, from April to June, 1977. Twenty-eight questions were clustered to form a profile of four major aspects of the sex industry: personal experience, offensiveness, visibility, and legality. A personal offensiveness scale was devised to measure more accurately the degree to which respondents were offended by various aspects of the industry. Interviewers' observations and the recorded respondent comments were incorporated into the data interpretation. Respondents were examined on their attitude toward the protections afforded by the First Amendment for purveyors of adult entertainments. This was crosstabulated with each respondent's evaluation of experience with adult entertainment to test for consistency in liberality or severity toward a particular kind of activity. Chi-square analysis at an .05 level of significance was then carried out. Respondents were asked several questions which gave them opportunity to indicate various possible solutions to the problem of regulating the sex industry, ranging from legislation to citizen action. Pearson correlation was applied to the independent variables of the age, education, and income of the respondents, with the offensive quotient as the dependent variable. A two-tailed t-test was done to determine whether geographic location of individuals in the survey population had an influence on their perception of visibility, offensiveness, and experience of the sex businesses in their midst. Scores from the questions representing the four areas would be totaled and divided to give quotients.  The quotients from Question 19 were ranked in order of seriousness.  Interviewers observations and the recorded comments of respondents were incorporated into the data analysis.(5)

Interview results were coded on IBM computer cards for analysis by the Statistical Package for Social Sciences (SPSS-G) on the IBM 370 computer located at John Jay College of Criminal Justice. Clusters of responses which could be statistically scrutinized were crosstabulated and received a chi-square to the .05 significance level.

## VI.  TRAINING OF STAFF

Interviewers received two sessions of training in survey techniques.  Two interviewers had been high school teachers who had changed careers to sociology and writing; four were practicing counselors; one was a former psychology professor who was beginning a private psychotherapy practice; one was a journalist and social worker. Interviewers were fluent in Spanish, French, and Italian, and administered the Spanish language questionnaires where necessary.  At the end of the interviewing phase, interviewers met with the director to give personal feedback on the experiences with respondents.  Interviewer-respondent gender was matched in almost all cases.

Survey staff was instructed to encourage all respondents to agree to a home interview, which the researchers judged the most suitable setting for the gathering of this type of information. An office was rented in the local YMCA to serve as an alternate interview locale for those respondents who preferred not to be interviewed at home.

# VII. SAMPLING BIASES

Limitations of time and financing allowed the researchers to include only two percent of the voters of the survey area in the project. On the average they were middle-aged and long-time residents of Clinton; therefore, it was expected that these respondents would present more severe opinions on the presence of adult entertainment operations in their neighborhood. There follows a comparison of selected population characteristics of the survey sample with those of the 1970 U.S. Census. See Table 2.2.

# VIII. SAMPLING TECHNIQUE

According to 1970 U.S. Census information, 20,929 people are living in the 16 square block Clinton area, the locus of the survey. On consulting maps of the 67thAssembly District and relevant 1970 Census tracts and voter lists, 6,700 names were gathered of those registered in the five political parties of the area. The 6,700 person voter list represented 32 percent of the total census population in the area. A systematic sampling process was employed, randomly choosing the first name from this list; then every 13th name thereafter, yielding an N=901. Four successive mailings to this number of people resulted in a total of 223, who indicated they would be interested in participating in the survey. Of this number, 155 interviews were successfully completed.

A profile of the sample population shows that 47.7 percent were male, 51 percent female. Eighty percent were White, the other 20 percent divided among Hispanics, Blacks, and Other. Mean age was 48.2 years; average length of education, 11.9

TABLE 2.2.

Comparative Census[6] and Survey
Sample Data

| (Per Cent) | 1970 Census | CTSS Sample |
|---|---|---|
| Sex | | |
| Male | 52.0 | 47.7 |
| Female | 48.0 | 51.0 |
| | 100.0 | 98.7 |
| Race | | |
| White | 88.0 | 80.0 |
| Black | 5.0 | 6.5 |
| Hispanic | N.A. | 11.6 |
| Other | N.A. | 1.3 |
| | | 99.4 |
| Marital Status | | |
| single/widowed/ separated | 49.4 | 58.4[7] |
| married | 45.5 | 28.6 |
| divorced | 5.0 | 9.1[8] |
| | 99.9 | 96.1 |
| Median Income | $7,485/yr. | $8,000-12,000/yr. |
| Median Length of Education | 10 yrs. | 11.9 yrs. |

years. Median income was between $8,000 - $12,000 per year. 54.5 per cent were single and/or widowed; 28.6 per cent were married; 16.9 per cent were separated or divorced. There was a wide scattering of occupation categories: of the eleven registered, the grouping were professional, 16.7 per cent; office worker 15.3 percent; performing arts 13.9 per cent; homemaker 13.2 percent. Average length of residence in Clinton was 21.1 years. 28 respondents reported 67 children among them, under age 17 and living in the household.

On April 15, 1977, a letter was mailed to each of the 342 enclosing a return postcard on which exact information was printed regarding an interview. The interviews gained from this mailing numbered 27. Two to three weeks after the mailing, follow-up by telephone was attempted. Phone calls to those who had listed numbers and who had not been heard from yielded 13 more interviews. Where the person could not be reached by telephone, two versions of postcards were mailed out: to those who did not have a telephone; and to those who had not returned a postcard and who did have a telephone. This effort yielded 6 interviews.

Continuing the same sampling technique, a second mailing to 327 people took place on May 17. Interviews from this mailing totaled 27. Follow-up phone calls several weeks later gave us 14 interviews. Because the postcard method of following up respondents not heard from did not seem to yield satisfactory numbers in the first mailing, it was decided to try personal visits as a method of follow-up, instead. This produced 13 interviews.

To further increase the number of respondents, a third mailing to 97 people on May 27 produced 9 interviews from returned postcards, 6 interviews from phone calls and 9 interviews from personal visits.

A final mailing to 135 people on June 17 yielded 16 interviews from returned postcards, 5 interviews from phone calls and 10 interviews from personal visits.

An office manager kept track of each attempt to contact a respondent and the result of that attempt, whether successful or unsuccessful. To this end a record of the entire survey operation was constructed on a large analysis pad, such as is employed for recording financial information. As each sampling took place, the names were recorded in alphabetical order and given a sequential number. Any phone calls, cards or personal visits to the person were recorded, as well as place, date of impending interview, name of interviewer, the date the questionnaire was returned and whether or not it was valid. The manager also undertook to dovetail the schedules of interviewers and respondents. In some cases this meant several changes of date which resulted in the loss of potential participants. At the end of the survey, a letter was sent each participant, thanking the person for taking part in the project and enclosing a card on which might be indicated the wish to receive a summary copy of the final report of the project. Of the 155 participants, 87 returned cards asking for a copy of the report.

A Spanish translation of the original letter was sent to each respondent whose surname on the voting list was Spanish. Response from this effort was poor. No postcards were returned from the Spanish mailings, although about twelve Spanish questionnaires were administered during the survey.

Table 2.3 shows the proportion of respondents who participated on their own initiative, after

TABLE 2.3.

Response of Sample Population to Initial Request to Participate in Survey and to Repeated Requests

Interviews granted from:

| | First Contact | | Follow-up Phone Calls | Follow-up Postcards | Personal Visits | (N) Total |
|---|---|---|---|---|---|---|
| | No. of People | Returned Postcards | | | | |
| Mailing I 4/15/77 | 342 | 27 | 13 | 6 | – | 46 |
| Mailing II 5/16/77 | 327 | 27 | 14 | | 13 | 54 |
| Mailing III 5/27/77 | 97 | 9 | 6 | | 9 | 24 |
| Mailing IV 6/17/77 | 135 | 16 | 5 | | 10 | 31 |
| TOTALS | 901 | 79 | 38 | 6 | 32 | 155 |

Breakdown of 901 contacted:   Interview valid 155
Interview Cancelled 68

Responded       223
No Answer        596
Letter Returned   82
                 901
                 ===

33

one contact from the survey office; and the proportion of those respondents who participated only after the second or repeated contacts from the researchers' office staff. In all, 901 voters made up the sample contacted. Of these, 155 granted interviews, making for a 17 per cent response rate.

Respondents were examined on their attitude toward the protections afforded by the First Amendment for purveyors of adult entertainment. Subsequent questions were grouped to lead the respondent to a consideration of the adult entertainment industry on a more pragmatic level, as he or she met up with it in its principal enterprises: adult film houses, massage parlors, live sex shows, bookstores and peepshows, and topless and bottomless bars. One question dealt with the public advertising of adult entertainments, observable to any passerby in Times Square streets. The offensiveness scale was utilized by respondents in answering these questions. By way of checking on respondents' observations on quantitative changes in the sex business in the area, a count of places of adult entertainment in the Times Square locale was undertaken at two different points in the time interval mentioned in Question 2.

Having elicited the respondent's evaluation of experience with adult entertainment in terms of offensiveness and liberality or severity towards this kind of business, several thought questions were presented by having the respondent consider hypothetical situations involving the degree to which x-rated entertainment might be shown in "family theaters", what they felt were legitimate grounds for harassing bookstores and theaters to force their closing; and a comparison of "O Calcutta" with a live sex show in terms of legitimacy of entertainment.

The next section of the questionnaire presented respondents with more considerations of x-rated entertainments, this time accompained by visual aids. Seven documentary photographs of a "typical" (9) massage parlor, x-rated film, live sex show, were presented for comment on these same establishments. All visual material was arranged in an album, and only one subject for viewing was shown the respondent at a time, so that judgment was not affected by any other consideration.

With respect to Question 11, despite the direction given "Interview Across" interviewers decided that it was best to question the respondent on his/her reaction to the photographs in a vertical manner; i.e., order a) to i) each of three separate instances, so as to minimize cumulative reaction to any one question. Positive statements were randomized among the negative ones to further prevent cumulative effects in responding. Statements like "this place has a right to be here" put the First Amendment question into specific, familiar, everyday context. The prediction implicit here is that there would be a different distribution of response to this question than there was to Question 1, although the issue is the same. To ascertain whether or not in fact more venereal disease and crime were brought into the area by these sex businesses, statistical information on the incidence of street crime and venereal disease was gathered from the Police Headquarters and from the New York City Board of Health.

Accompanying the next section were nine actual magazine covers of publications sold on newsstands in the area. Presented one at a time from the album to the respondent, they elicited a "Yes" or "No" answer as to whether or not the magazine should be publicly displayed on local newsstands.

Some photographs of record album covers were taken from a collection of 40 slides shown as a program given by Women Against Violence Against Women(10), a California-based feminist group. These photographs and others made up the visual accompaniment to Question 13, which explained that these were record albums designed to sell to a teen-age market in the Times Square area, and sought respondents' opinion of each one.

Other titles were gained by the researchers themselves as follows: five teenagers ranging in age from 17 - 19 years were asked to go to several Times Square record stores and to choose rock n' roll records which they themselves might purchase for their personal listening pleasure. Thus, covers which were relatively "neutral" from those which were anti-feminist were photographed and included for respondent viewing. All covers were presented as being sold to teenagers in the area. Covers where female abuse was the message were alternated with more innocuous ones purchased by teenagers to lessen the impact of the former covers on the respondents destined to view them during the survey.(11)

Several questions in the final section of the questionnaire gave respondents opportunity to register their opinion on a sample "ballot" dealing with New York City Planning Commission proposals which had been put forward just previous to the start of the survey in April 1977.

The issues were zoning for "adult" businesses, legalizing the sex entertainments, and decriminalizing prostitution. In a question dealing with a group of adult entertainments and activities related to them, the respondent was presented with six possible remedies which might be applied, and was instructed to indicate one or more solutions for each activity presented.

In order to ascertain what visibility local leaders had in the minds of respondents, they were asked to consider a list of 9 people who had taken public stands on the question of adult entertainment in the area, and asked to rate each one on his/her performance on the question. The last question asked the respondent to rank the three most serious problems which in his judgment were related to the adult entertainment industry in Clinton-Times Square.

Demographic questions were reserved for the end of the interview. A question on the religious affiliation of the respondent was omitted because it was thought that the mere designation of a religious denomination would not reveal enough about religious influence on attitude toward public sexual entertainments and advertising thereof. A cluster of questions would have to be constructed and presented in order to ascertain this properly. Because the questionnaire was already deemed long by critics, this variable was omitted from the study.

A cue card was presented to the respondent with varying levels of annual income on it, and he/she was asked merely to state the letter which preceded the income level corresponding to their reply. Interviewers were instructed to record sex and race from observation.

## FOOTNOTES

1. See Appendix I for exact delineations of the Clinton and Times Square areas.

2. See map, Appendix I.

3. 3rd New International Edition (1971)

4. Black's Law Dictionary, West Publishing Co., (1968) P. 1215.

5. See Appendix IV.

6. 1970 Census of Population and Housing. U.S. Bureau of the Census, Pt. 1,2,3. May 1972.

7. figures not available

8. Marital status categories differ from those infra so as to facilitate comparison with 1970 Census figures.

9. One of the researchers, also a resident of the area, walked around the Times Square neighborhood and selected the establishment on the basis of its typifying the adult entertainment business in question.

10. A part of the Feminist Women's Health Center, 1112C Renshaw Blvd., Los Angeles, California. Known as WAVAW, the group gained some measure of publicity in 1977 when it threatened the WEA Record Company with a national boycott if a series of advertising posters for the Rolling Stones' album "Black & Blue" were not taken down from California roadsides. Success in this effort was followed by a national lecture tour

showing dozens of slides of rock album covers
featuring women in various states of sexual
abuse and torture.

11. The section dealing with the record album covers
has not been incorporated in the final report
as the responses to the question were inconclusive.

CHAPTER III

THE COMMUNITY'S RESPONSE TO
THE ADULT ENTERTAINMENT INDUSTRY

The satisfaction of the nuisance definition, in New York State, requires the plaintiff to show that the conduct or display complained of is indecent or offensive to the senses. With this in mind, an offensiveness scale was designed for the respondent to use in answering Question 3, which asks for a rating of nine different adult entertainment businesses in Times Square; and Question 4, which asks for a rating of nine related activities of adult entertainment as they are personally experienced on the streets of the area. Thus, an offensiveness rating was obtained from each individual on the adult businesses themselves, and on the public manifestations of the sex industry as experienced by anyone using the streets of the Clinton-Times Square neighborhood.

In Question 3, the lowest mean offensiveness(1) was for bookstores(5.9) while the highest rate was for prostitutes approaching passersby(7.8) in Table 3.1. The overall mean, 6.7, indicates that respondents exhibited a medium degree of offensiveness when considering sex businesses per se. Low ratings (0-2) were given even when reservations were expressed about the possibility of advertising or materials seen by children; when they were thought more humorous than offensive; and when it was thought that the individual offering was inoffensive, but the concentration of all adult entertainment activities was not. These comments suggest that "offensiveness" has social as well as personal implications for these respondents. Some comments suggest that offensiveness is related to the style of the deviant operation in question: in the high rating for massage parlors (a) and street prostitution (d), respondents indicate that "they reach out" and that this is "aggressiveness". This tends to corroborate Kirkpatrick's theory regarding the style of deviance.

TABLE 3.1.

Generalized Mean Offensiveness Ratings of Principal
Times Square Adult Entertainment Activities.

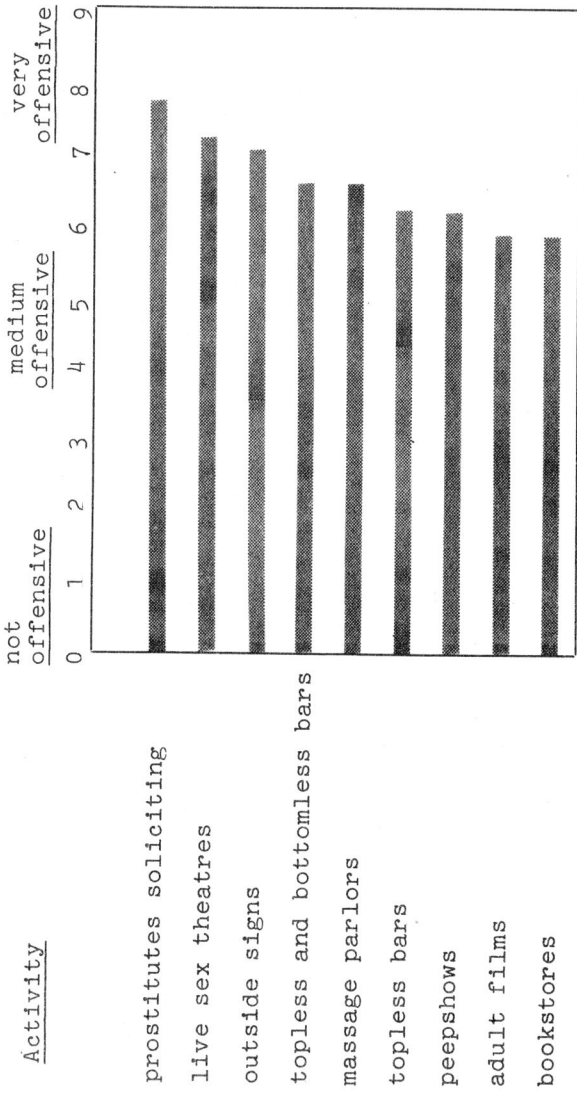

| | not offensive | | | | medium offensive | | | very offensive | |
|---|---|---|---|---|---|---|---|---|---|---|
| Activity | 0 | 1 | 2 | 3 | 4 | 5 | 6 | 7 | 8 | 9 |
| prostitutes soliciting | | | | | | | | | | |
| live sex theatres | | | | | | | | | | |
| outside signs | | | | | | | | | | |
| topless and bottomless bars | | | | | | | | | | |
| massage parlors | | | | | | | | | | |
| topless bars | | | | | | | | | | |
| peepshows | | | | | | | | | | |
| adult films | | | | | | | | | | |
| bookstores | | | | | | | | | | |

Overall Mean = 6.686

Since Question 4 deals with personal experience of the pornography trade, the overall experience offensiveness mean, 7.5, is higher than the generalized offensiveness mean for Question 3, 6.7. Six of the items in Question 4 are related to street prostitution or massage parlor activity, and this may account for the higher means, given the higher ratings in Question 3 for the same two items. Ratings of "9" were given by people who commented that they associated prostitution with the particular activity, or that they had had painful personal experiences with solicitation by prostitutes. Ratings of "1" or "2" were given in some cases for the following reasons: "never see it here" "not really aware of this" and "not so many here". Again, this seems to indicate that personal experience of the activity accounts for higher ratings. Medium or lower ratings on the offensiveness scale could also be the result of a reticence to admit the existence of a problem.

In summary, what offends respondents most as expressed by the items given the highest offensiveness ratings in Questions 3 and 4 are activities connected with street prostitution which are highly visible to the resident or passerby in Clinton streets.

Question 11 was an indirect means of measuring offensiveness by testing what respondents are willing to believe about places of adult entertainment. Respondents were shown several photographs of each of three "adult" establishments which are typical Times Square establishments in terms of street visibility. Only the front of each building was photographed; i.e., a view which would be that of any passerby.

43

TABLE 3.2.

Mean Offensiveness Ratings of Times Square Adult
Entertainment Activities as Experienced on Streets.

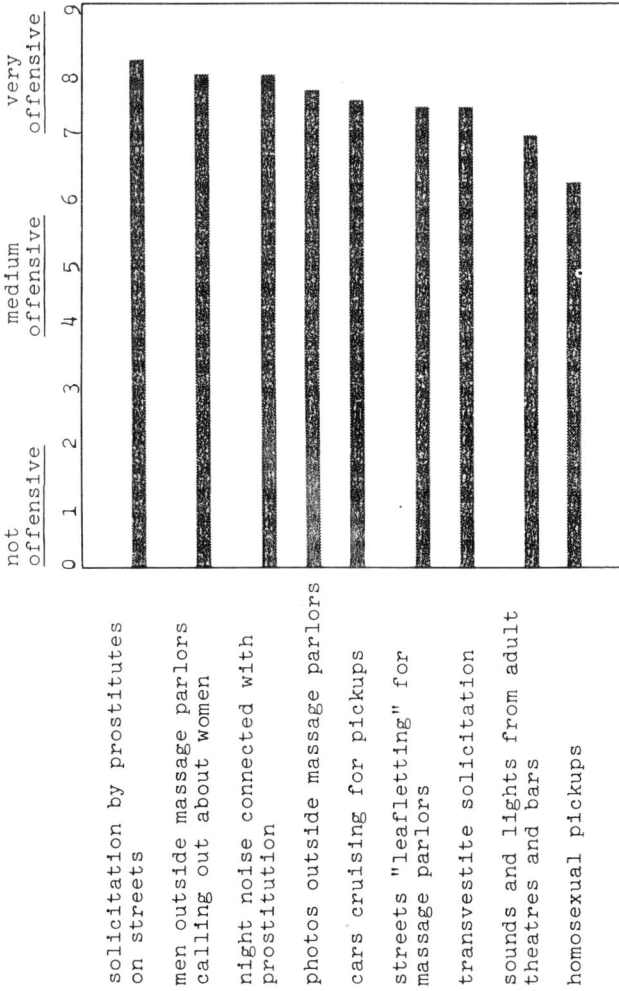

| | not offensive | | medium offensive | | | very offensive | |
|---|---|---|---|---|---|---|---|
| | 0 1 2 3 4 5 6 7 8 9 | | | | | | |

solicitation by prostitutes on streets

men outside massage parlors calling out about women

night noise connected with prostitution

photos outside massage parlors

cars cruising for pickups

streets "leafletting" for massage parlors

transvestite solicitation

sounds and lights from adult theatres and bars

homosexual pickups

Overall Mean = 7.541

TABLE 3.3.

Offensiveness Ratings of Times Square Street Prostitution

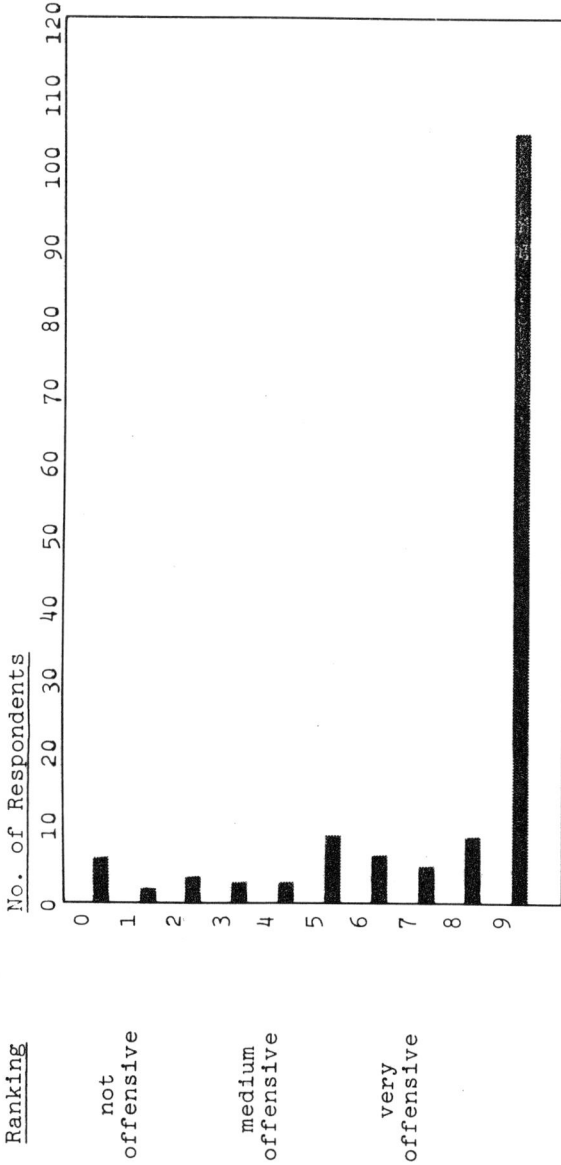

Mean Rating: 7.792

Future events were to prove the choice of all three places of adult entertainment a propitious one. Shortly after the photos were taken, each establishment received its share of public attention from either government officials, City corporation counsel, or private groups.

During the survey, which was in progress at the same time as the Mayoral campaign, the theater "Show World" located on 8th Avenue between 42nd and 43rd Streets, received wide publicity when as a candidate for re-election, Abraham Beame, personally visited it and announced to the press that he then and there decreed that it be closed down. Within 24 hours, a judge had declared this action unconstitutional and ordered the establishment opened again. "Show World's" owner explained his case to the press and this also received a good deal of media coverage, including the fact that he had stepped forward to save a venerable Chelsea neighborhood theatre (an area adjoining Clinton) by purchasing it. At the same time, he was planning to feature "family" entertainment in the old Elgin movie house.

It was also during the survey that wide public attention was accorded the issue of using children as young as three years of age for "adult" photographs and films. Under the leadership of Judi-Ann Densen-Gerber, who founded Phoenix House, demonstrations against this practice were mounted in front of 42nd Street bookstores and peepshows, with the result that books and films featuring young children were removed (temporarily) from the shelves. This is some of the related publicity which was being carried on at the same time the photographs of the "typical" X-rated film were being shown to respondents. The film advertised on the marquee in the photos is "Intimate Teenagers".

The massage parlor chosen to be photographed for
the survey album was "Pillow Talk" and it has the
most dynamic history in terms of street visibility.
It is located at 1173 Avenue of the Americas,
between 45th and 46th Streets, has a peep show-
bookstore operation on the first floor which also
sells x-rated film loops, and an "Encounter"
parlor on the second floor. Until recently, it
was the only adult establishment on the Avenue
between 42nd and 59th Streets. On the sidewalk in
front of 1173 are several men distributing leaflets
advertising the "Encounter" or second floor part
of the business, sometimes calling attention to
the presence of the women by announcing "all nice
girls up there". Pairs of men stand at each
corner of the block leafletting for the parlor.
While photographing this place for survey purposes, one of the researchers was threatened by
one of these "leafletters". Various signs cover
the front of the four-story brownstone building,
including a "For Sale" sign which has endured many
changes in window display. From April to May 31,
1977, the single window on the ground floor of this
establishment was covered with about a dozen large
photographs of scantily-clad females in provocative
poses, and gave all the appearance of a medium-
tawdry adult materials store. Revolving lights
on the awning had the visibility of about five
blocks in a north-south direction along the Avenue.
Loud music usually emanated from the door to the
second floor. In the same block about four doors
to the south, is a "Burger King" which is noted as
a culinary mecca for innumerable school children's
groups on field trips to the Rockefeller Center
area. The School of Performing Arts(2) is within
a block of the massage parlor.

TABLE 3.4.

Offensiveness Ratings of Times Square Massage Parlors.

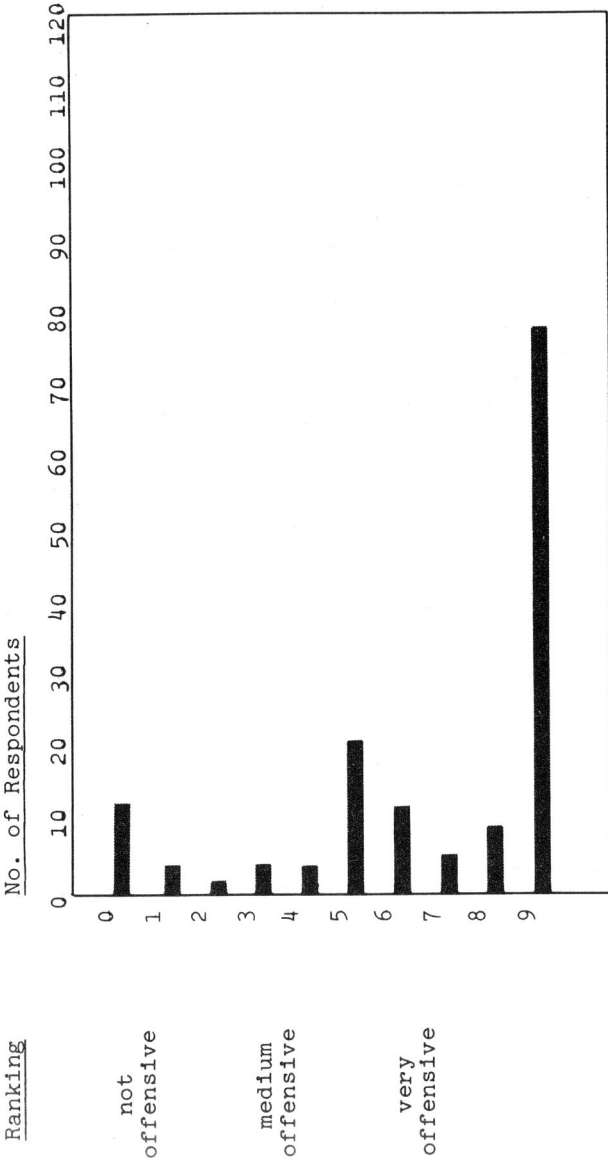

Ranking

No. of Respondents

not offensive

medium offensive

very offensive

Mean Rating: 6.724

In April, a three-day "Spotlight on Smut" rally
was held at 42nd Street and Broadway. Sponsored by
Mayor Beame's Midtown Citizens' Committee, it
featured celebrities, sports figures, and promi-
nent community realtors voicing suggestions on how
to "clean up" the area. 8,000 people attended the
final rally. Early June 1977 saw the content of
the photos in the window at 1173 escalated in
X-terms: now appeared gargantuan thighs and breasts
in contorted poses with a female face somewhere
in the background. Appropriate black triangles
had been applied to the photos. It was during this
phase that a researcher observed a kindergarten
class reacting as it passed before the parlor window: screams, pointing, and covering of faces,
as they trudged their way to "Burger King".(3)

As the mayoral campaign intensified, so did
various candidates' pronouncements bemoaning the
state of pornography in Times Square. During this
time there were more manifestations of official
and public outrage which amounted to pressure on
existing sex establishments. About 1500 residents
of Holy Cross Parish demonstrated in front of selected massage parlors along the portion of Eighth
Avenue known as "the Minnesota Strip" they were
equipped with bullhorns into which they shouted
"Tear It Down".(4) The Mid-Town Law Enforcement
Project headed by Sidney Baumgartner, received
some publicity as it attempted to close down
some of the more tawdry massage parlors on
Eighth Avenue. The Police Department also received attention in its attempts to cut down the
distribution of "kiddie porn" movies by posing
as potential customers, then arresting dealers on
42nd Street.

By early July, the photographs at 1173 were
covered with brown wrapping paper for a period

TABLE 3.5.

Offensiveness Ratings of Signs Outside Places of
Adult Entertainment in Times Square.

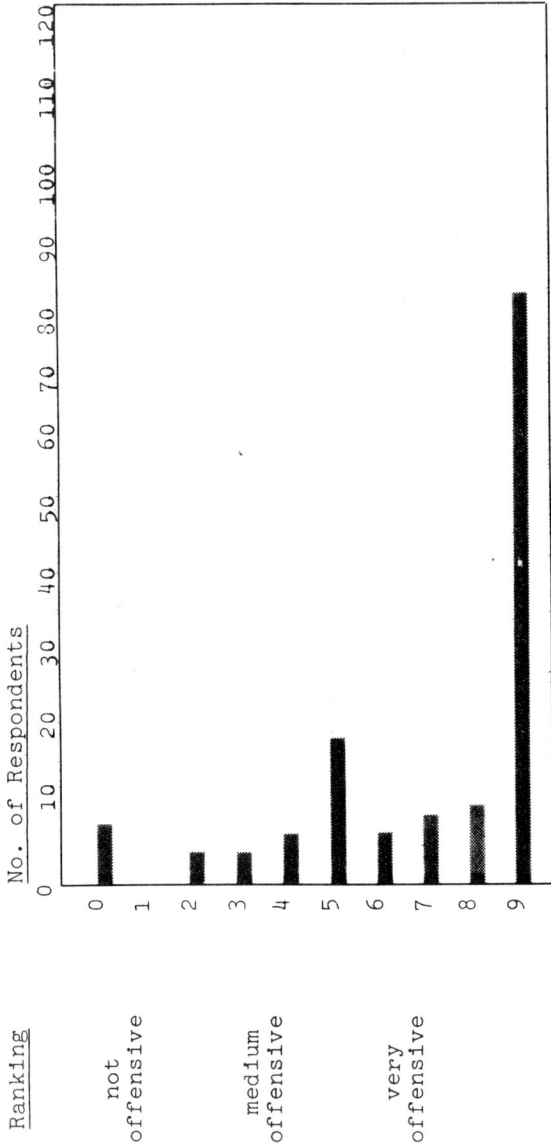

Mean Rating: 7.181

TABLE 3.6.

Offensiveness Ratings of Topless and Bottomless
Bars in Times Square.

No. of Respondents

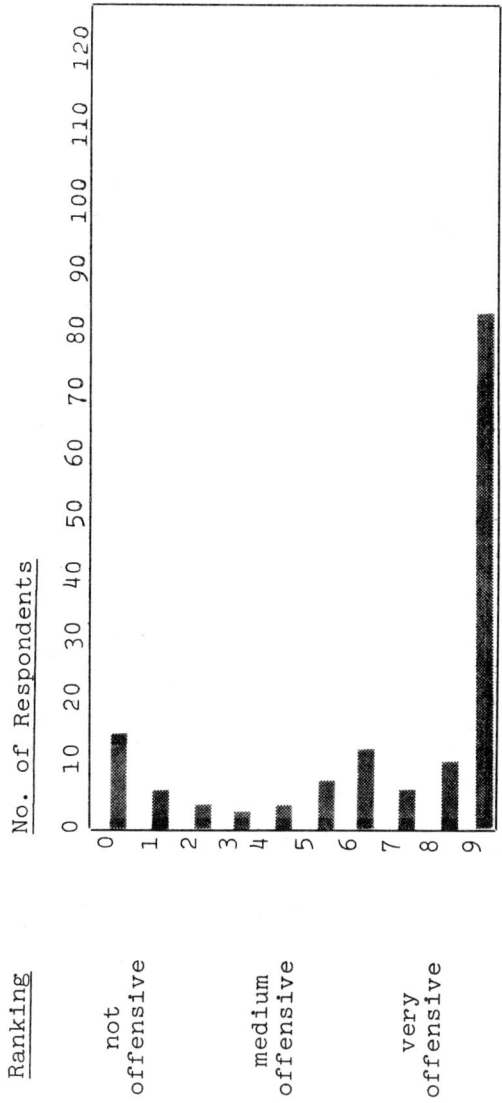

Mean Rating: 6.687

of about three weeks. This coincided with the
tenure of the Democratic National Convention at
Madison Square Garden. During the entire period
April - November, 1977, various men stationed in
front of the store and on the two corners of
West 45 and West 46 Streets and the Avenue were
distributing leaflets advertising activities on the
2nd floor of 1173, sometimes calling out about
the women upstairs to passersby. At this writing,
the men are still there; recently, one was heard
to remark "These damn Kids" - thereby showing some
sensitivity to the presence of the patrons of
"Burger King".

In the fall of 1977, a suit, <u>City of New York</u>
v. <u>1173 Sixth Avenue Bldg. Co., Inc.</u>, brought a
preliminary injunction temporarily restraining the
defendants from maintaining and permitting the
maintenance of prostitution and a public nuisance(4)
at 1173 Sixth Avenue. To this date, that action
is still pending. In December, 1977, a wooden
door with a padlock was installed outside the stair-
way which had led up to the "Encounter" part of the
operation and where about eight women had been
working. The street leafletting ceased. Several
weeks later, this door was open again, this time
decorated with Christmas lights and painted signs
advertising "Girls". Christmas lights blinked in
the third story of the building. Apparently, the
"Encounter" operation had recouped its forces one
flight up. Street leafletters once again took up
their positions on the block.(5) The Mid-Town
Enforcement Project, a part of the Mayor's Task
Force, is now considering whether or not it is
appropriate to initiate another suit, or to continue
to press the old action. Meanwhile, the display
window on the ground floor has reverted to a more
austere display style: Since about November, 1977,

TABLE 3.7.

Offensiveness Ratings of Live Sex Theatres in Times Square.

No. of Respondents

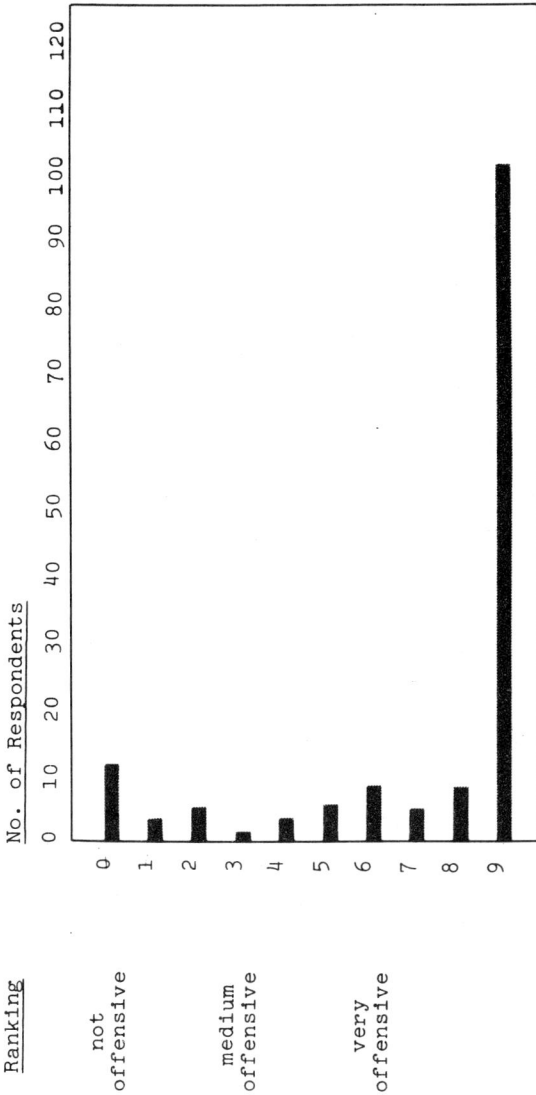

Mean Rating: 7.405

the lurid photos have disappeared, to be replaced with a plain red neon sign "Peep Show, 25¢". Farther down the block at the corner, an adult bookstore has opened and is operating Spring, 1980.

Between 55-60 per cent of respondents agreed that the live sex and film theatres "looked like a fire trap", while 71.3 per cent agreed to this statement after viewing the massage parlor photographs. An average of 85 per cent agreed that all three places brought about an increase in area traffic. From the wording of the comments which accompanied responses to this question, it appears that respondents believe that patrons of X-rated entertainments do not come from the area itself.(6)

For the question "it brings venereal desease into the area", about 74 per cent of the respondents agreed to this when applied to the live sex and film theatres, but when viewing the massage parlor photos, 83.8 per cent agreed with the statement. As a number of massage parlors in the Times Square area are known to be fronts for prostitution activities, the escalation of agreement is not surprising, since venereal disease is associated with massage parlors. The high rate of agreement with the first two statements needs more discussion. The 74 per cent who agreed to the venereal disease statement as it applied to the first two establishments may have had in mind a casual relationship between exposure to pornographic experience and sexual activity, where venereal disease might be contracted or transmitted; or that a significant number of patrons attracted by these kinds of entertainment were themselves already infected by venereal disease.

TABLE 3.8.

Respondents' Reactions after Viewing Photographs of
Fronts of Three "Typical" Times Square Adult
Entertainment Businesses. Expressed in percentage.

| Visibility Impact | Live Sex Theatre "Show World" Agree/Disagree | | Film: "Intimate Teenagers" Agree/Disagree | | Massage Parlor Agree/Disagree | |
|---|---|---|---|---|---|---|
| a. this place looks like a fire trap | 56.0 | 30.5 | 58.1 | 26.5 | 71.3 | 14.7 |
| b. this business brings jobs into the neighborhood | 17.4 | 80.5 | 14.7 | 82.7 | 16.0 | 82.0 |
| c. it brings more traffic into an area already congested | 85.4 | 9.3 | 84.8 | 10.6 | 86.8 | 8.6 |
| d. it brings venereal disease into the area | 75.7 | 19.6 | 73.3 | 20.5 | 83.8 | 9.5 |
| e. this place has a right to carry on business here | 33.3 | 66.0 | 32.5 | 66.2 | 31.8 | 66.2 |
| f. this place affects real estate values in the immediate area | 96.7 | 2.0 | 96.7 | 2.0 | 95.9 | 3.4 |
| g. it attracts undesirable loiterers who interfere with everyday business of Clinton residents | 95.4 | 3.9 | 95.4 | 3.3 | 93.4 | 5.3 |
| h. people want this service or it would not be there | 56.7 | 40.7 | 53.0 | 45.0 | 55.3 | 42.8 |
| i. it brings more crime into the neighborhood | 88.2 | 10.5 | 89.5 | 8.6 | 90.2 | 7.8 |

In recent years, nationwide reports on the incidence of venereal diseases indicate that they have
reached epidemic proportions in America. It would
seem that the respondents' perceptions regarding
the increase of venereal disease in the Clinton-
Times Square area are affirmed by the Department of
Health's Bureau of Health Statistics and Analysis.(7)
Health Areas 4500, 4700, and 5200 overlap the demographic parameters of this study.(8)

It should be noted that the researchers, in
dealing with the City Board of Health, learned the
difficulty of pinpointing the origin of venereal
diseases by health area. Reasons for this are:
a) the infected person prefers to remain anonymous
because a certain social stigma is still attached
to these diseases. Thus, the person will go for
treatment where he or she is not known: to a dis-
tant clinic or a large center such as the City
venereal disease clinic at 29th Street and Ninth
Avenue; b) because names, addresses and other per-
tinent information on persons who have contracted
a communicable disease is required in reports to
the City Board of Health, private physicians have
been less than candid in reporting cases of venereal
disease which have come to their personal attention
for diagnosis and treatment; c) venereal disease
and sexual promiscuity probably have a high correlation in many cases and the person simply cannot remember or know where the disease might first
have been contracted.

Statement f): "this place affects real estate
values in the immediate area" received the highest
degree of consensus of any item in the question.
About 96 per cent of the respondents agreed with
this statement. The strength of agreement may
have been due to the fact that the meaning of the

TABLE 3.9.

Incidence of Principal Venereal Diseases by
Health Area, Borough of Manhattan 1973-1976.
(Dept. of Health)

| Health Area* | 1973 Syphilis/Gonorrhea | | 1974 Syph./Gon. | | 1975 Syph./Gon. | | 1976 Syph./Gon. | |
|---|---|---|---|---|---|---|---|---|
| 4500 | 37 | 142 | 36 | 218 | 69 | 273 | 58 | 324 |
| 4700 | 63 | 295 | 92 | 338 | 93 | 383 | 92 | 476 |
| 5200 | 77 | 545 | 100 | 553 | 88 | 612 | 103 | 651 |

*Partial overlap with study area

57

question is dual: real estate could be affected positively or negatively, according to how one viewed adult entertainment activity: lucrative in itself, being able to pay high rentals which drove out smaller neighborhood businesses; or engendering such a tawdry, run-down atmosphere as to discourage the presence of other businesses in the immediate vicinity, eventually contributing to the decline of real estate values of the particular block in question. Respondents have a strong conviction of the dynamic power the adult entertainment industry exerts on real estate in the area.

Item g): "it attracts undesirable loiterers who interfere with everyday business of residents of Clinton" received an almost equally high consensus: 94.5 per cent agreed with this statement as it applied to all three businesses. Because the question contained two statements, it is not possible to ascertain whether agreement represented consensus on both items. What is clear is that the respondents view the sex establishments as places which attract patrons who are socially "undesirables".

For the statement i): "it brings more crime into the neighborhood", about 89 per cent of the respondents agreed this to be true for all three businesses. Like all other large urban areas which attract a high number of social "undesirable," Times Square is associated in the public mind with a high crime rate.

The researchers attempted to verify if in fact the crime rate had increased in the survey area between January 1973 and January 1976. They met with difficulties similar to those encountered while correlating the venereal disease statistics for reliability. Individual police precincts no longer keep statistics: this process has been computerized at central Police Headquarters in lower Manhattan. Several Precinct boundaries overlap the survey area. As of May 5, 1972, Mid-Town North comprised Lexington Avenue to the Hudson River between 43rd and 59th Streets, while Mid-Town South comprised Lexington Avenue to Ninth Avenue, between 29th and 45th Streets. While there are drawbacks in analyzing data from such a large area, which includes two other loci of high sexual activity: Penn Station and Murray Hill, some crime statistics are set down for the midtown precincts in Table 3.10 for the period 1973-1976.

Arrests for prostitution tripled in Mid-Town South between 1973-1976 and increased by about 400 in Mid-Town North. However, one must be aware that these arrest figures are not totally representative of the prostitution problem. For example, if one pimp oversees 15 girls, each expected to earn a minimum of $200 nightly at $10 to $20 a "trick", one pimp is responsible for 150 assignations per night. When one multiplies this by the number of pimps, and nights in the year, it is easily seen how arrest statistics do not reveal the true picture.

In addition, pressures from the leaders of the municipal government and the legitimate theatre industry have increased the volume of midtown prostitution arrests to the point where prostitution can no longer be treated as a misdemeanor. Instead, prostitutes taken off the streets are simply charged with disorderly conduct, kept at the police station house overnight, and released the following day.(11) Therefore, the information released by the police regarding arrest statistics for the two Precincts in Table 3.10 is not reliable. Prostitution activity in Times Square is several times what is recorded on official records.

TABLE 3.10.

Selected Arrest Statistics for 3-Year Period in Midtown New York. NY Police Headquareters Data.

| | ARRESTS | | | |
|---|---|---|---|---|
| | Mid-Town 1973 | South 1976 | Mid-Town 1976 | North 1976 |
| **Prostitution** | | | | |
| Prostitution (Misd.) | 476 | 1,382 | 1,078 | 1,409 |
| Permitting (Misd.) | 8 | 18 | 18 | 4 |
| Patronizing (Viol.) | 10 | 70 | (not avail.) | 24 |
| **Obscenity** | | | | |
| Obscenity 2° (Misd.)[1] | 382 | 193 | 114 | 130 |
| Offensive Display of Material (Misd.) | 123 | 0 | 6 | 3 |
| Public Lewdness (Viol.)[2] | 89 | 125 | 22 | 39 |
| **Sex Crimes** | | | | |
| Rape (Fel.) | 44 | 29 | 14 | 19 |
| Sexual Abuse 2° & 3° (Misd.) | 21 | 60 | 8 | 15 |
| **Larceny** | | | | |
| Grand (Fel.) | 807 | 2,867 | 284 | 691 |
| Robbery (Total) | 969 | 1,141 | 360 | 457 |
| **Drugs** | | | | |
| Sale of Controll. Sub.(Fel.) | 203 | 673 | 107 | 35 |
| Posses. " (Fel.) | 141 | 899 | 92 | 102 |
| Posses. " (Misd.) | 492 | 1,287 | 265 | 155 |

Under the term "obscenity", arrests for offensive public display went to zero in Mid-Town South and were insignificant in Mid-Town North; however, there has been notable increase in public lewdness in both precincts during the three-year period. Sex crimes reported do not seem to be very numerous. There has been a significant rise in the rate of incidence in the various types of street thefts and in transactions involving drug trafficking as noted in Table 3.10.

While studies done for the Presidential Report on Pornography and Obscenity in 1970 concluded that there is no direct relationship between pornographic entertainment and anti-social behavior, the analysis of 11 i) shows that in the minds of the respondents, there is still an important connection to be made between the two phenomena.

Analysis was done on statements 11 b), e), and h) which tended to justify the presence of the three businesses in Times Square. In 11 b), "this business brings jobs into the neighborhood", an average 15.5 per cent of all respondents for the three items agreed with this statement. It is not clear why this represents the lowest degree of agreement for all items in Question 11. Disagreement with the statement may reflect the fact that while some residents of the area do work from time to time in X-rated enterprises,(12) there is still a social stigma attached to such activities,(13) and respondents may not be eager to divulge a personal connection with them. The ephemeral nature of "adult" operations would also facilitate this kind of secretiveness.

The second item, 11 e), "this place has a right to do business here" directly correlates with Question 1, which asks in the abstract whether a sex business has a right to be where it is in the photograph. About 33 per cent of those asked agreed with the statement, as opposed to the 49.3 per cent who replied "Yes" to Question 1. Sixteen per cent of the respondents changed their First Amendment stand from positive to negative when viewing pornographic activity in an everyday, familiar context. The context is emphasized because the very word "here" in 11 e) brings the X-rated business into the area itself. It is interesting to conjecture what the response would have been if the question had been worded "this place has a right to carry on business".

The question of place as significant in the operating of adult entertainment activities is demonstrated in 11 h): "people want this service or it would not be there". About 55 per cent of respondents agreed with this statement; and about 43 per cent disagreed, indicating that the response to the question was the most controversial. Six of eleven comments recorded by interviewers on Question 11 had to do with this item; three of the six comments indicated that it was "not the residents" who wanted these entertainments. The comments which agreed that people did indeed "want this service" indicated that it did not have to be where the respondent lived. The researchers conclude that in the minds of respondents, demand for sex entertainments and the satisfaction of their potential customers is to be tolerated but it should be carried on in such a way as not to constitute a nuisance to the neighborhood.

Question 5 dealt with the respondent's attitude toward a series of sexual activities as they might be depicted in a film scene. This was the most probing question regarding personal tolerance of sex publicly displayed. Descriptions of six scenes were printed on a cue card to avoid heightening

62

TABLE 3.11.

Respondents' Attitude Toward A Film Scene
Depicting Various Sexual Activities.

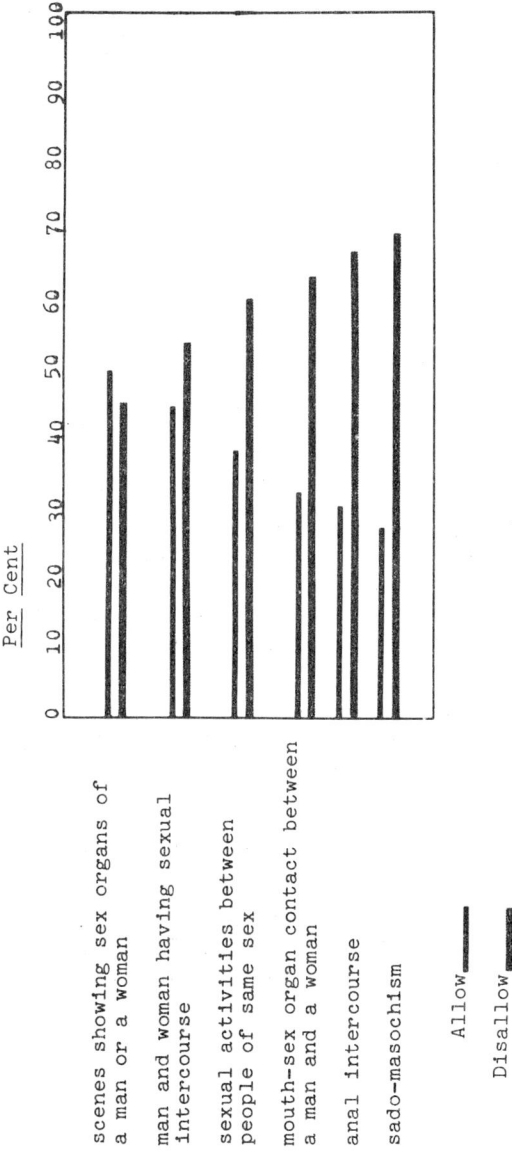

Per Cent

scenes showing sex organs of
a man or a woman

man and woman having sexual
intercourse

sexual activities between
people of same sex

mouth-sex organ contact between
a man and a woman

anal intercourse

sado-masochism

Allow ▬▬▬

Disallow ▬▬

63

any embarrassment the respondent might have felt with the question, and to screen out the interviewer's role as much as possible in dealing with responses. Replies were compiled in two categories of "allow" and "not allow". (See Table 3.11.) The responses ranged from 45.8 per cent who felt that showing the sex organs in a film should not be allowed to 71.1 per cent who felt that sado-masochistic activities should not be allowed in a movie. The only filmed sex scene which more people felt should be allowed in some greater degree than not allowed was: "scenes which show the sex organs of a man or woman": 49.7 per cent of the respondents thought this should "definitely" or "probably" be allowed.

The comments recorded with "allow" responses to this question show a concern regarding its effect on others: "While they might be o.k. for most, I don't know if they have a bad effect on some". Those who would allow these film scenes also have an appreciation of the right of adults to see whatever they wish: "...o.k. because they can be seen in private". Some who answered "Don't Know" also employed the privacy issue: "since I don't have to be subjected to it, I don't care what they have in it".

The following data demonstrates the respondents' perception of the intensity of the adult entertainment industry in the Times Square area during the year preceding the entire survey period, April-June, 1977. They were asked: "...which activities do you think are more visible in the community this past year; that is, since January, 1976?"

In all cases, over 80 per cent of the respondents said that they noticed "More" or "No change" regarding sex businesses during the past year, and

TABLE 3.12.

Respondent Perception of Changes in Intensity of
Adult Entertainment Businesses Over a One-Year Period.

| | Visible in Community | | |
| | More since 1976 | Less since 1976 | No change |
|---|---|---|---|
| a. Films | 70.9 | 4.1 | 25.0 |
| b. Live sex theatres | 69.6 | 7.2 | 23.2 |
| c. Peep shows | 68.3 | 4.2 | 27.5 |
| d. Signs outside places of adult entertainment | 65.3 | 5.4 | 29.3 |
| e. Prostitutes approaching passerby | 58.7 | 18.0 | 23.3 |
| f. Massage parlors | 58.2 | 8.9 | 32.3 |
| g. Bookstores | 57.5 | 8.9 | 33.6 |
| h. Topless and bottomless bars | 45.3 | 11.1 | 43.6 |
| i. Topless bars | 43.5 | 13.0 | 43.5 |

18 per cent or less for all items said fewer "adult" businesses existed in the area during the past year. A judgment of the strength of the presence of places of adult entertainment over a period of time is difficult for several reasons.

1. Landlords of low rent property in decaying areas of Clinton are attracted to adult entertainment businesses because these enterprises are inclined to bring in high rentals. They occupy the premises for a period of time until the property is no longer suitable, or the business is harassed to move. The landlord may then abandon the building, and it is then taken over by the City for renovation or demolition. The adult business relocates, usually not too far away; and the degree of itensity of sex businesses in Times Square makes it possible to mask the closings and openings by combining forces with already existing businesses, or moving to another floor of the same building. A case in point is the massage parlor "Pillow Talk", located at 1173 Avenue of the Americas, whose visibility history is sketched more fully elsewhere in this report.(14)

This phenomenon operates even on 42nd Street, usually thought of as having a high concentration of long-term pornographic entertainments. At present, the 42nd Street Redevelopment Corporation is sponsoring, among other renovations along 42nd Street, the Theatre Row Project, located between 9th and 10th Avenues on that street. According to Fred Papert, President of the non-profit Corporation, its goal is redevelopment of the section between Broadway and 12th Avenue, with the obvious effect of displacing adult entertainment businesses.(15)

2. Confusion regarding criteria for closing pornographic businesses leads to events such as the brief closing of the live sex theatre "Show World" in the spring of 1977 by then-Mayor Abraham Beame. Twenty-four hours later, a judge declared this action unconstitutional and ordered the premises opened once again. Given the rapidity with which the sex businesses move from place to place, some respondents may be perceiving frequency of relocation as "More" when in point of fact there has been no change. Those who say "less" on the other hand, may be seeing places close but are unaware of others opening in the same area.

Table 3.13 represents the only available information on actual numbers of X-rated establishments between 6th and 10th Avenues and 38th and 57th Streets. This is the area which the Mid-Town Planning Office considers "Times Square". As only one set of figures was available from that office on Times Square places of adult entertainment, for purposes of comparison, one researcher attempted a "walking count" of the five principal sex businesses in the same area, one year later. It can be seen from Table 3.14 that there has been a drop in every category, particularly in massage parlors. It is of significance that although numerically this type of establishment is nowhere as numerous as peepshows or films, yet it is the massage parlor operation which respondents have selected for the higher offensiveness ratings in Questions 3 and 4.

Question 6 evoked a significant severity response from participants on what they felt was allowable in the realm of public advertising of sexual entertainments. Table 3.14 presents respondents' ranked order of acceptance of public advertising of adult entertainments.

TABLE 3.13.

Sex Oriented Establishments in Times Square Area
by Principal Type over a One-Year Period[1]

| | Mid-Town Planning Count as of 1/1/77 | Researcher Walking Count as of 12/31/77 |
|---|---|---|
| Peepshow/Bookstore | 39 | 22 |
| Live sex shows | 10 | 6 |
| Topless Bars | 12 | 7 |
| Adult Film Houses | 35 | 28 |
| Massage Parlors | 33 | 9 |

[1]The time period given for participants of the survey to consider
was from January 1, 1976 to June, 1977.

TABLE 3.14.

Respondents' Attitude Toward Advertising for
X-Rated Entertainments and Street Prostitution.

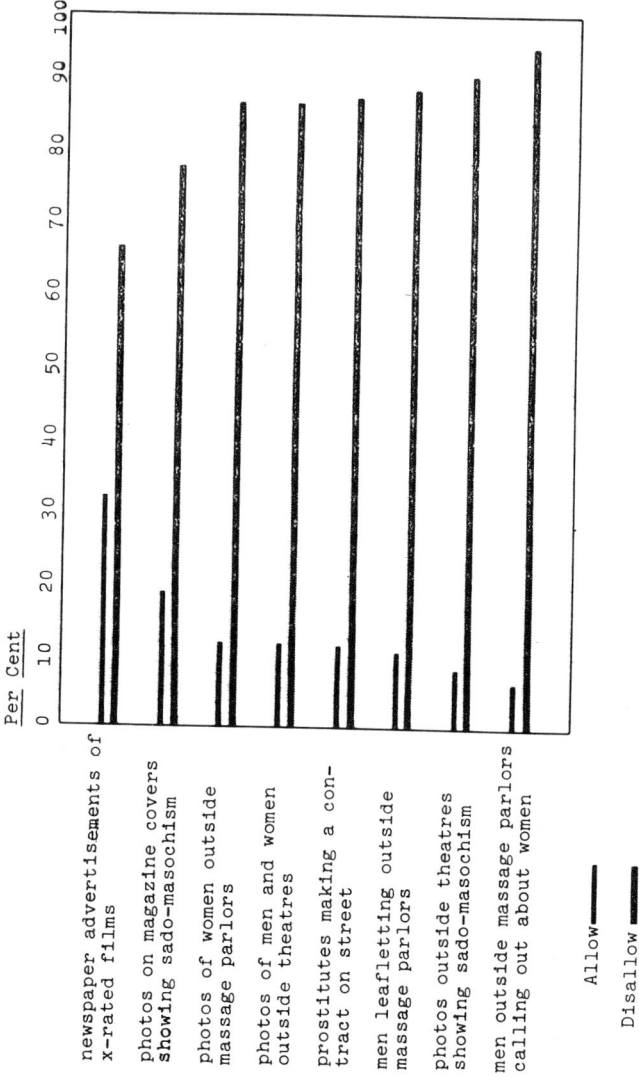

Per Cent

| | 0 | 10 | 20 | 30 | 40 | 50 | 60 | 70 | 80 | 90 | 100 |

newspaper advertisements of
x-rated films

photos on magazine covers
showing sado-masochism

photos of women outside
massage parlors

photos of men and women
outside theatres

prostitutes making a con-
tract on street

men leafletting outside
massage parlors

photos outside theatres
showing sado-masochism

men outside massage parlors
calling out about women

Allow ▬

Disallow ▬

69

Highest ratings were given questions dealing with sado-masochism or prostitution. Over 90 per cent of respondents felt that advertising for these activities should not be allowed as a street phenomenon. The most favorable ratio applied to the question regarding newspaper advertising for sex entertainments: while 33.2 per cent felt it was all right, 66.3 per cent did not think it should be allowed.

## "YOU CAN'T TELL A BOOK BY ITS COVER"

The respondents were shown actual covers from nine magazines exhibited and sold on area newsstands between April and June, 1977. The table below is arranged in ascending order of acceptance of the covers, which may bear no relationship to the contents of the magazine itself. Of the nine magazines, only "Playboy", "Playgirl", and "Penthouse" were acceptable to over 50 per cent of the respondents for exhibition on newsstands. "OUI" received 49 per cent approval and the same amount of rejection. Over 80 per cent of those asked rejected "Screw" and "Pleazure" as appropriate for public viewing.

Low percentage of acceptance for "Screw" and "Pleazure" brought with it various comments from respondents, indicating a "strong no" concerning public viewing of these two publications. Some suggested they be available only in certain bookstores; or that the publication of these two magazines be subjected to an "obscenity tax".

Finally, to determine community solidarity on the visibility and offensiveness factors of the adult entertainment industry, the respondents were grouped into quadrants: northeast (NE), northwest (NW), southeast (SE), and southwest (SW).

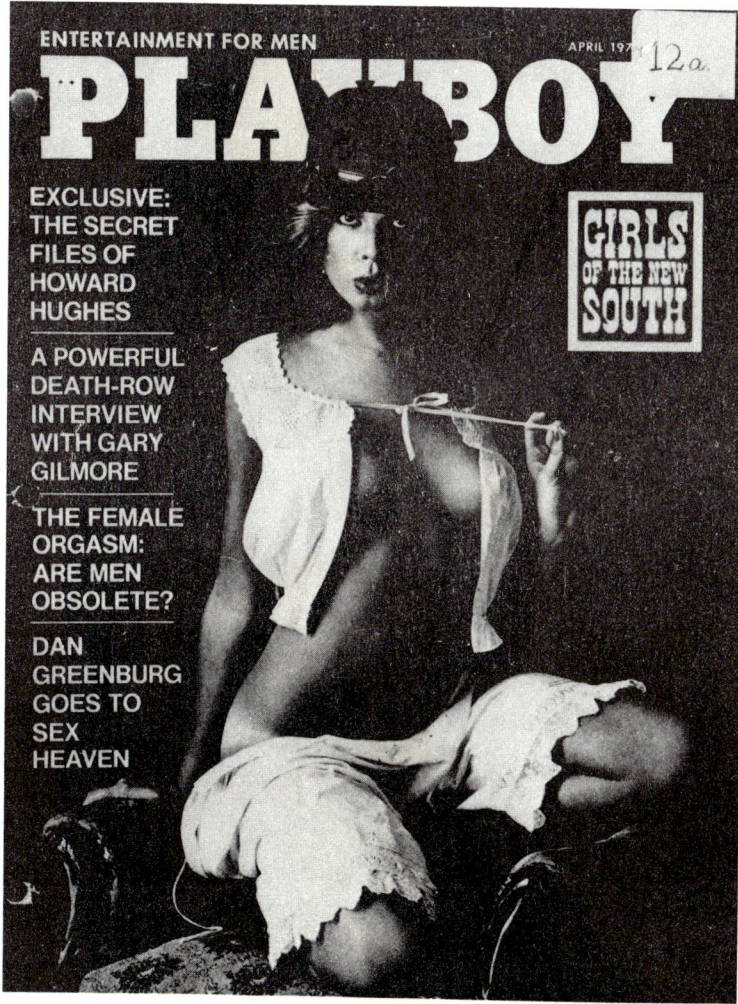

Reprinted with permission of PLAYBOY
©April, 1977

OUI

APRIL, 1977.

72

Reprinted with permission of Jeff Dunas,
Penthouse Magazine.

Reprinted with permission of HUSTLER Magazine,
a Larry Flynt Publication.

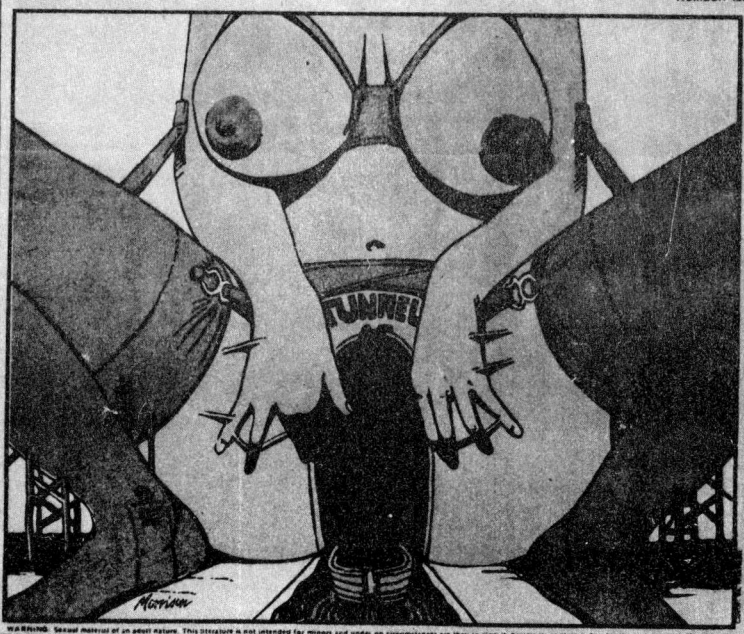

Reprinted from SCREW, an Al Goldstein publication.
Copyright 1977 by Milkyway Productions, Inc.

Copyright Release Unobtained

76

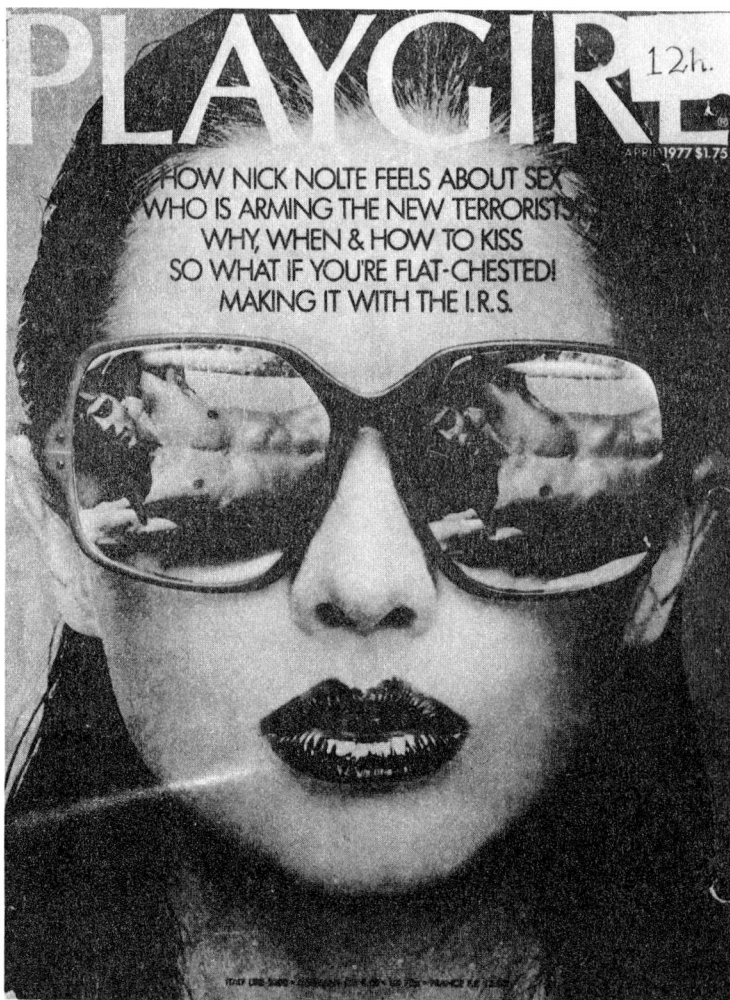

Reprinted with permission Playgirl Magazine
(c) April 1977

Reprinted with permission of CHIC Magazine,
a Larry Flynt Publication.

TABLE 3.15.

Responses after Viewing Covers of Nine Selected
Adult Magazines Displayed in Times Square Area.

| Magazine/Issue | O. K. for Display on Area Newsstands. | |
|---|---|---|
| April/May 1977 | YES | NO |
| Screw | 15.5 | 82.6 |
| Pleazure | 16.1 | 81.3 |
| Affair | 21.9 | 76.1 |
| Chic | 34.4 | 63.0 |
| Hustler | 41.6 | 56.5 |
| Oui | 49.0 | 49.0 |
| Playboy | 51.6 | 45.2 |
| Penthouse | 59.7 | 39.0 |
| Playgirl | 63.9 | 34.2 |

The central north-south dividing line was 9th
Avenue, from West 38th to West 54th Streets. Since
the population concentrations are not uniform
throughout the survey area (see map, Appendix III)
the respondents were grouped in approximately equal
numbers east and west of 9th Avenue, and then
divided into northwest and southwest groups and
northeast and southeast groups. Hence there is
no specific line which divides the survey area
into north and south segments.

Respondents were grouped according to the
quadrants. The means of questions 2, 3 and 4 were
submitted to a two-tailed probability t-test, to
see if a) there was any disparity in community
standard and b) if those who lived more closely
to the adult entertainment industry might be more
affected by its pressure. The first analysis was
done on subjects residing east of 9th Avenue. The
extremes were used; i.e., those who lived furthest
away and those closest to the center of the sex
businesses. The results show no significant difference in recognition of visibility, offensiveness
or experience. Apparently the northeast and southeast subsamples are equally offended and see the
same level of activity whether or not they reside
near the core of the industry.

The west side of 9th Avenue was examined on the
same basis as the east side of the Avenue. As can
be seen from Table 3.17, there was a significant
difference in the quotient designed to measure the
level of visibility or change between January 1,
1976 and the survey period. The respondents who
were in the northwest quadrant saw the greatest
change in the level of visibility of the adult
entertainment industry. This group saw the increase
to be more dramatic than those nearer to the center
of the activity, namely, the southwest quadrant.

TABLE 3.16.

T-Test of East Geographic Extremes of Sample by
Visibility, Offensive and Experience Means.

| Geographic Location | Question | No. of Cases | Mean | 2-Tail Probability T-Test |
|---|---|---|---|---|
| NE SE | 2) Visibility | 21 16 | 3.67 4.13 | 0.471 |
| NE SE | 3) Offensiveness | 21 16 | 8.12 7.32 | 0.298 |
| NE SE | 4) Experience | 21 16 | 6.15 5.15 | 0.198 |

TABLE 3.17.

T-Test of West Geographic Extremes of Sample by
Visibility, Offensiveness and Experience Means.

| Geographic Location | Question | No. of Cases | Mean | 2-Tail Probability T-Test |
|---|---|---|---|---|
| NW | 2) Visibility | 31 | 3.01 | 0.049 |
| SW | | 27 | 3.71 | |
| NW | 3) Offensiveness | 31 | 8.02 | 0.078 |
| SW | | 27 | 7.28 | |
| NW | 4) Experience | 31 | 5.59 | 0.191 |
| SW | | 27 | 4.83 | |

Researchers were confronted with evidence that the section of the sample which experienced the highest sensitivity toward the visibility of the sex businesses on 42nd Street lived furthest from that area.

This fact is made less perplexing, however, when it is recalled that: 1) the intensity of the adult entertainment trades and the speed of openings and closings of individual businesses make it difficult for those living in its midst to accurately assess its total volume at any one time. Those living close to but outside the locus of sex businesses are more aware of the totality of movement of the industry: for instance, some respondents living on the northern edge of the survey territory expressed fears because some peepshows and bookstores have now moved up to blocks in the 50's. A case in point is 1465 Broadway. The 42nd Street Redevelopment Corporation purchased the ground floor at 1465 in June, 1977, which housed the largest peepshow in Manhattan, and converted it to a Police Substation and Information Center. The peepshow/bookstore successfully relocated northwards, giving ground to the fears expressed in responses to Question 19 that the "adult" establishments are beginning to settle in the 50's streets. 2) neighborhood deterioration was the problem connected with the adult entertainment industry which was given the most negative ranking in Question 19, and deterioration is naturally more to be feared in newly-reconstructed neighborhoods than in the ones closer to 42nd Street, which are still in a more advanced state of urban decay.

Both the northwest and southwest groups were equally offended on the scales connected with Question 4 and 5, regardless of whether they were close to the center of the activity or further away.

## Summary

Offensiveness. For the satisfaction of the nuisance definition in New York State, it is important to show that the conduct or display complained of is indecent or offensive to the senses. With this in mind, an offensiveness scale was designed for each respondent to use in answering two questions; one which asked for a rating of nine different adult entertainment businesses in the Times Square area, and the second presented nine related activities of these businesses as they are personally experienced on the streets of Clinton. The scale weighted responses as follows: 0-3 none or low offensiveness; 4-6 medium offensiveness; 7-9 high offensiveness.

Computer analysis of the questions asking for offensiveness ratings of the nine sex businesses yielded the lowest mean offensiveness for bookstores (5.9), while highest was for prostitutes approaching a passersby (7.8). The overall mean for the nine businesses was 6.6, indicating that respondents exhibited a medium degree of offensiveness when considering sex establishments per se. None or low offensiveness ratings (0-3) were given even when reservations were expressed about the possibility of children seeing sex advertising or other materials; when the adult activities were thought more humorous than offensive; and when it was thought that the individual sex entertainment was inoffensive, but the concentration of all adult entertainment activities was not. These comments suggest that "offensiveness" for these respondents is a reaction to pornography which has social as well as personal implications. Some comments suggest that offensiveness is related to the style of the deviant operation in question: in the high rating for massage parlors (7-9) and street prostitution, respondents indicate that "they reach out" and that this is "aggressiveness."

The overall offensiveness mean for the questions dealing with personal experience of nine street activities related to pornographic businesses was 7.5. Six of the nine items in this question which received highest offensiveness ratings (above 7.5) were related to street prostitution or massage parlor activity. Low ratings or noᴗ offensiveness was indicated in some cases because it had never been observed in the respondent's neighborhood, or had occurred there only rarely. This seems to confirm that personal experience of a pornographic activity results in higher offensiveness rating. Medium or lower ratings on the offensiveness scale, according to some interviewer's comments, could also be the result of a reticence to admit the existence of a problem in a respondent's block or neighborhood.

Offensiveness was measured indirectly by a question testing what respondents are willing to believe about places of adult entertainments. Respondents were shown several photographs of the fronts of a massage parlor, an adult film house, and a live sex show, typical of their kind in terms of street visibility. Some of the more significant results are: an average of 85 per cent of respondents agreed that all three places brought about an increase in area traffic. About 74 per cent of those surveyed agreed that the live sex and film theater brought more venereal disease into the area, but when viewing the massage parlor photos, those who agreed with the statement rose to 83.8 per cent. The highest degree of consensus of any item in the question was accorded to the fact that the sex establishment affected real estate values in the area: 96 per cent agreed with this. The strength of agreement might be due to the fact that it is a dual question: real estate values could be affected positively or negatively by adult businesses. 94.5 per cent agreed with the statement in regard

to all three businesses; that they brought undesirable loiterers who interfered with everyday
business of Clinton residents. About 89 per cent
of respondents agreed that all three establishments bring more crime into the area. From the
wording of the comments which accompanied responses
to this question, it appeared that respondents
believe that patrons of x-rated entertainments do
not come from the area itself. Also noteworthy
are three items in this question which justified
the presence of the three businesses in Times
Square. The lowest degree of agreement was given
to the statement: "This business brings jobs into
the area" - 15.5 per cent of all respondents agreed
with this statement as it related to all three
places. Disagreement with this statement may reflect the fact that while undoutedly some area
residents do work from time to time in x-rated
enterprises, and respondents may not be eager to
divulge a personal connection with them. For the
statement "This place has a right to be here",
about 33 percent answered in the affirmative regarding all three places. It should be kept in
mind that in the first question of the survey interview, 49.3 per cent replied in the affirmative
when asked whether adult entertainment businesses
had a constitutional right to operate.

The question of place as significant in the
operation of adult entertainment activities is
demonstrated in the third statement "People want
this service or it would not be there". About 55
per cent agreed with this statement; 43 per cent
disagreed, making it the most controversial item.
Of eleven comments recorded by interviewers on this
question, six had to do with this item; three of the
six comments indicated that it was "not the residents"
who wanted these entertainments. However, comments
which agreed that people did indeed "want this
service" indicated that it did not have to be where
the respondent lived. The researchers conclude that

in the minds of respondents, demand for sex entertainments and the satisfaction of their customers is to be tolerated, but it should be carried on in such a way as not to constitute a nuisance to the neighborhood. From the examination of direct and indirect measurements of offensiveness, it can be said that the respondents are moderately to highly offended by the presence of the adult entertainment industry in the Clinton-Times Square area.

Visibility. Respondents were asked to express their awareness of whether nine activities related to adult businesses had become more or less visible in the area during the preceding year; that is, 1976-77. The activities were massage parlors, films, bookstores, prostitutes on the street, signs outside sex establishments, topless bars, bottomless bars, live sex theatres, and peep shows. In all cases, over 80 per cent of the respondents said that they noticed "more" or "no change" regarding sex businesses during the past year, and 18 per cent or less for all items said fewer adult businesses now existed in the area.

However, a judgment on the strength of the presence of adult businesses over a time period is difficult for several reasons. 1) Landlords of low rent properties in decaying areas of Clinton-Times Square attract adult businesses because they bring in high rentals. When the property is no longer suitable, or harassed to move by city agencies, the landlord may abandon the building. The adult business relocates, usually not too far away; but the degree of intensity of sex businesses in the area makes it possible to mask closings and openings by combining forces with already existing businesses, or moving to another floor of the same building. A case in point is the massage parlor "Pillow Talk" at 1173 Avenue of the Americas, which moved its massage parlor operation to the third

floor after a court order closed the second floor
massage enterprise. It has now been forced to close
the third floor parlor. The men leafletting on
the street are also gone, and all that remains is
a rather austere red and green neon sign proclaiming
"25 cents, Peep Show" in its front windows. 2)
Confusion regarding criteria for closing pornographic businesses leads to events such as the
brief closing of the live sex theatre "Show World"
in the Spring of 1977 by then-Mayor Abraham Beame.
Twenty-four hours later, a judge declared this action
unconstitutional and ordered the premises opened
once again. Given the rapidity with which the sex
businesses move from place to place, some respondents
may be perceiving frequency of relocation as "more"
pornography when in point of fact there has been
no change in the number of places. Those who say
"less", on the other hand, may be seeing establishments close down, but are unaware that other places
are opening in the same area.

An attempt was made to compare actual counts of
x-rated businesses between 6th and 10th Avenues and
38th and 57th Streets during the year 1976-77.
This is the area which the Midtown Planning Office
considers "Times Square", and includes the entire
survey area. Only one set of figures was available
from this office, so for comparison purposes, one
researcher attempted a "walking count" of the five
principal sex businesses in the same area, one year
after the date of the Midtown count. It was
found that there had been a drop in numbers of every
adult category, particularly the massage parlors.
It is significant that although numerically, this
type of establishment is nowhere as numerous as
peepshows or films, yet it is the massage parlor
which respondents have selected for the highest
offensiveness ratings in the questionnaire.

When presented with a list of public advertising activities of sex entertainments, those interviewed were severe in what they felt was allowable in this realm. Over 90 per cent of the respondents felt that advertising for prostitution and sado-masochistic activities should not be allowed as a street phenomenon. The most favorable ratio applied to the question regarding newspaper advertising for sex entertainments: while 33.2 per cent felt it was all right, 66.3 per cent did not think it should be allowed.

The respondents were shown actual covers from nine magazines exhibited and sold on area newsstands between April and June, 1977. Of the nine publications, "Playboy", "Playgirl" and "Penthouse" were acceptable to over half the respondents for public newsstand exhibition. Over 80 per cent of those asked rejected "Screw" and "Pleazure" as appropriate for public viewing.

To determine the degree of community solidarity on the offensiveness and visibility factors of the adult entertainment industry, the respondents were grouped into four quadrants based on geographic place of residence. The number of respondents in each quadrant was approximately equal to the others. The appropriate statistical analysis was applied (2-tail t-test) to see if those who lived more closely to the center of the adult industry might be more affected by its pressure. In the analysis done on the north-south quadrants on the east side of Ninth Avenue, there was no significant difference in recognition of visibility or offensiveness; apparently, the northeast and southeast subsamples are equally offended, and perceive the same level of activity, whether or not they reside proximate to the industry's core. When the west side of Ninth Avenue was examined on the same basis, there was a significant difference in the quotients designed to measure the level of visibility of adult entertainment businesses between January 1, 1976 and the survey period. The respondents in the northwest quadrant saw the greatest change in level of visibility. This group saw the increase to be more dramatic than those in the southwest quadrant, who are nearer to the center of adult activity. Although it was theorized and found that high visibility would correlate with high offensiveness, researchers were confronted with evidence that the section of the sample which experienced the highest sensitivity toward the visibility of the sex businesses on 42nd Street lived furthest from that area. This result is made less perplexing, however, when it is recalled that the intensity and speed of openings and closings of adult entertainments make it difficult for those living in its midst to accurately assess its total volume at any one time. Those living in the northwest quadrant are more aware of the totality of the industry's movement. Some respondents living in the northern quadrants of the survey territory expressed fears because some peepshows and bookstores have moved up to blocks in the 50's streets. Furthermore, in a question asking respondents to rank in order of seriousness a number of community problems related to the pornographic trade, neighborhood deterioration was ranked the number one problem. Deterioration is naturally more to be feared in the northwest quadrant where there is some new construction and no visible sign of pornography. Neighborhoods closer to 42nd Street are still in a more advanced state of urban decay, and already experience high saturation of sex businesses.

Both the northwest and southwest groupings were equally offended when asked to consider listings of adult businesses and related street activities, regardless of their location in relation to the pornographic trade.

In studying the phenomenon of the northwest quadrant's awareness of the presence of sex businesses in the 42nd Street area, researchers also conjecture that these residents are "rendered insecure in their use of property": the fourth component of a nuisance in this State. This kind of response would also indicate that the northwest area respondents see more clearly a threat to their own lifestyle when made to consider the slow encroachment of entertainments not yet present in their midst, but known to be slowly relocating northward.

# FOOTNOTES

1. Mean offensiveness was used because in every case from Question 3a)-3h) and Question 4 a)-4i) the median offensiveness figure was approximately one point higher.

2. At 120 W. 46 St.

3. 1173 is now a coffee shop.

4. New York TIMES Monday, Nov. 15, 1976

5. In the case People v. Remeny the N.Y. State Court of Appeals on July 13, 1976 declared it unconstitutional to restrain street leafletting, as it was an infringement of First Amendment liberties.

6. See infra p. 54

7. Department of Health, City of New York, Bureau of Health Statistics and Analysis. Vital Statistics by Health Areas and Health Center Districts 1973, 1974, 1975, 1976.

8. See Appendices I and II for Clinton-Times Square Survey map and health areas.

9. N.Y. Criminal Practice. Jas. Zett., Vol. 10 (1976). 235.05. A person who, knowing its content and character 1) promotes or possesses with intent to promote, any obscene material or 2) produces, presents, or directs an obscene performance or participates in a portion thereof which is obscene or which contributes to its obscenity.

10. ibid. 245.00. A person who intentionally exposes the private or intimate parts of his body in a lewd manner or commits any other

lewd act a) in a public place, or b) in
private premises under circumstances in which
he may readily be observed from either a
public place or other premises, and with
intent that he be so observed.

11. From an interview on Jan. 25, 1977 with an
officer at the Mid-Town North station house
who was charged with enforcing prostitution
law.

12. In the proposed Zoning Plan of the City Planning Commission which was defeated in the City
Council in the Spring of 1977, provision was
made to zone all aspects of sex entertainments
with the notable exception of live sex theatres.
An opinion on this omission came to the attention of the researchers: members of the
legitimate Broadway acting profession take jobs
in sex shows from time to time when they are
unemployed. A pastor in a local Christian
church confided to one of the researchers that
some young girls in the parish had admitted to
taking jobs as "go-go" dancers to earn money.

13. See respondents' comments in the analysis of
Question 10.

14. See this Chapter, pp. 52 and 55.

15. CHELSEA-CLINTON NEWS 2/9/78.

CHAPTER IV

THE FIRST AMENDMENT PRINCIPLE
AND THE ADULT ENTERTAINMENT
INDUSTRY IN CLINTON

The complexity of the First Amendment's role in the articulation of a definition of obscenity has been thoroughly discussed, as had been the previous efforts at delineating a "community standard" faithful to _Miller_. In this part of the study, the results of the generalized First Amendment question: "You may know that most owners and operators of adult entertainment businesses claim the right to provide their services under the First Amendment to our Constitution, which guarantees freedom of speech and the press. Do you agree with this stand?" will be examined and cross tabulated with the survey population's response to specific activities expressive of both a presumed First Amendment right and a potentially pornographic activity. What we shall attempt to discern is if there is any significant shift in respondents' positions from their generalized First Amendment stand - for or against the question posed above and their specific responses to explicit forms of potentially pornographic activity.

I.  THE GENERAL FIRST AMENDMENT POSITION

When asked as a matter of principle "Do you agree with this stand?" regarding the owners of adult entertainment businesses' claim to a right to provide these services, the responses split 49.3 per cent for this right and 50.7 per cent against it. The near-perfect dichotomy shows that the survey population's understanding of the First Amendment right in the abstract on the adult entertainment issue is controversial.(See Table 4.1.)

There is no overall agreement on its meaning. The fact that the respondents were so evenly divided makes it all the more imperative that an attempt be made to examine and clarify their understanding of what the expression of adult entertainment implied constitutionally. Such an analysis helped the researchers establish a standard of acceptability

TABLE 4.1.

First Amendment Right Of Owners to
Provide Adult Entertainment

| Question One on First Amendment | Agree YES | Disagree NO | Total |
|---|---|---|---|
| (Per Cent) | 49.3 | 50.7 | 100.0 |

or a "community standard" on the constitutionality of such activities as were presented to the respondents for consideration as expressive of what comprises the adult entertainment industry.

Methodologically, the generalized First Amendment question was asked as the first question in the survey to stimulate the respondent's thinking on the question of adult entertainment as a mode of expression and to record the general attitude respondents had to freedom of expression. The presentation of this as the initial question also prevented any cumulative effect on the respondents as they were asked detailed questions later. Nor was the respondent re-examined again on this issue. The generalized position initially articulated was tested against the specific responses given to the ensuing questions.

## II. ANALYSIS OF SELECTED DATA WITH FIRST AMENDMENT POSITION

Researchers selected replies from four questions whose content would be crosstabulated with respondents' position toward constitutional protection for the operators of sex businesses, as expressed in Question 1. The questions chosen were: Question 5, which elicits responses to sexual entertainments in a private viewing context; Question 8, which presents various grounds for closing down pornographic businesses on grounds other than obscenity; Question 11, which gathers respondents' opinions on three typical Times Square adult businesses, and Question 16, which allows respondents to vote on legislative and judicial proposals dealing with adult business. The results for each question were submitted to chi square ($x^2$) analysis to test the significance of First Amendment position when applied to specific situations involving the operating of adult entertainment businesses. To avoid unnecessary repetition in the remainder of this report, those respondents who adhered to First Amendment protections for owners and operators of sex businesses will be known as "Group A", and those opposed to this principle will be known as "Group B".

Table 4.2 presents the results of the cross-tabulation of Questions 1 and 5. For greater simplicity of analysis, the four response categories of Question 5 were collapsed into "allow" and "not allow". "Don't Know" responses were eliminated from calculations.

The only filmed sex scene which a majority of Group A found acceptable was the one showing sex organs of men or women. They do not object in the main to a mere depiction of the private parts of human bodies in a film. The sexual activities described in b) - f) in this question did not receive majority approval of the "liberal" element in the sample population as fit subjects for filming and private viewing.

For Group B, the reaction was just the opposite: 65.2 per cent did not approve of showing sex organs in a film scene. For the behavioral items, the disapproval ranges from 68.9 per cent of Group B to 90.5 percent of the group.

Results in Table 4.2 are arranged by declining personal acceptance of the various sex scenes in all four response categories. The attitude of Group B was predictable; it is the response pattern of Group A that demonstrates the conservative nature of the respondents on what is a private sex enter-

## TABLE 4.2.

First Amendment Position and Reaction to a list of Filmed Sex Scenes.

| Scenes Showing | I Amendment % YES- Group A | Allow | Don't Allow | I Amendment % NO- Group B | Allow | Don't Allow |
|---|---|---|---|---|---|---|
| a. sex organs of man or woman | 49.3 | 71.2 | 28.7 | 50.7 | 34.7 | 65.2 |
| b. male-female intercourse | 49.0 | 60.6 | 39.4 | 51.0 | 31.1 | 68.9 |
| c. homosexual activity | 49.3 | 56.3 | 43.7 | 50.7 | 21.9 | 78.1 |
| d. oral sex | 49.0 | 50.7 | 49.3 | 51.0 | 20.3 | 79.7 |
| e. anal intercourse | 48.6 | 50.0 | 50.0 | 51.4 | 16.2 | 83.8 |
| f. sado-masochism | 49.3 | 47.2 | 52.8 | 50.7 | 9.5 | 90.5 |

tainment, experienced only by a willing audience with no perceptible impact on street life of Clinton.

The total negative response pattern regarding whether filmed scenes of sexual activity should be allowed is better understood when one considers the high mean offensiveness ratings given by all respondents to Question 3 and 4 to items associated with prostitution activities, live sex shows, and massage parlors, all of which involve personal interaction.

Question 8 asked how the respondent would feel if law enforcement officers harassed bookstores or film theatres by closing them down on grounds other than obscenity. As the analysis for Question 8 was not included in Chapter 3, the overall response percentage appears below.(See Table 4.3.)

Table 4.4 gives the results of the first option for the closing of certain sex businesses for false advertising. The results of the chi-square are not significant. This means that both groups felt that false advertising was indeed a legitimate reason for law enforcement personnel to close these establishments as such advertising does violate the Administrative Code. Group A, or the First Amendment proponents, feel that false advertising would be acceptable grounds for closing these establishments, while on the other hand, Group B would probably accept any reason for closing these establishments.

The second rationale offered to the respondents for the harassment of adult entertainment establishments was lack of air space. (Question 8b). There was a significant difference between the two groups on this option for closure. Fewer of Group A

101

TABLE 4.3.

Per Cent of Respondents Accepting Violations
as Basis for Closing Sex Businesses

| Possible Violation | Agree | Disagree | Row Total |
|---|---|---|---|
| a. False Advertising | 81.7 | 16.3 | 98.0 |
| b. Lack of Air Space | 82.4 | 17.0 | 99.4 |
| c. Non-Compliance with Fire Code | 91.6 | 7.1 | 98.7 |
| d. Inadequate Sanitary Facilities | 83.8 | 14.9 | 98.7 |
| e. Unlicensed Service Personnel | 83.2 | 13.4 | 96.6 |

TABLE 4.4.

First Amendment Position and Attitude
Toward Closure for False Advertising

| First Amendment Right to Free Expression | Close Bookstore/Movie on Grounds of False Advertising | | |
|---|---|---|---|
| Per Cent | Agree | Disagree | Row Total |
| Group A YES 49.3 | 77.1 | 23.0 | 100.1 |
| Group B NO 50.7 | 86.8 | 13.1 | 99.9 |
| Column Total 100.0 | | | |

$$x^2 = 0.2183$$

TABLE 4.5.

First Amendment Position and Attitude
Toward Closure for Lack of Air Space

| First Amendment Right to Free Expression | Close Bookstore/Movie for Lack of Air Space | | Row Total |
|---|---|---|---|
| | Per Cent | Agree | Disagree | |
| Group A YES | 49.3 | 75.7 | 24.3 | 100.0 |
| Group B NO | 50.7 | 90.8 | 9.2 | 100.0 |
| Column Total | 100.0 | | | |

$$x^2 = 0.0248$$

respondents (24.3%) believed that lack of air space was a sufficient reason to close such establishments. However, Group B felt this was sufficient reason for closure (90.8%). These findings are consistent with the manner in which survey Question 1 was answered. Group A was not going to accept "lack of air space" a relative term, to close or infringe on the businessman's right to operate. These differences as shown in Table 4.5 were significant to the .02 level.

The third rationale that was offered to the respondents for the harassment of adult entertainment establishments was non-compliance with the fire code. The difference that was obtained on this question was not significant at the .05 level. Both groups felt that this was a legitimate reason for closing an establishment that dealt with adult entertainment. Group A did not feel that they had the right to endanger the lives of patrons by non-compliance with the fire code; Group B felt that this was sufficient grounds for closing the business. (See Table 4.6.)

The fourth rationale that was offered to the respondents for the harassment of this industry was "lack of sanitary facilities". Both groups felt that this was a legitimate reason for the harassment of sex establishments. However, there was a significant difference on the strength of this agreement. Group A indicated that sanitary facilities were an insufficient reason to close these establishments. The significance level for Table 4.7 was .01.

The significance of Table 4.7 lies in the respondents' skepticism regarding an adequate rationale for closure. While the specifics of false advertising and non-compliance with the fire code are demonstrable by administrative law, the health regulations are less precise in this area. The respondents' sophistication in discerning probable

TABLE 4.6.

First Amendment Position and Attitude Toward
Closure for Possible Violation of Fire Code.

| First Amendment Right to Free Expression | Per Cent | Violation of Fire Code Agree | Disagree | Row Total |
|---|---|---|---|---|
| Group A YES | 49.7 | 89.4 | 10.7 | 100.1 |
| Group B NO | 50.3 | 96.1 | 3.9 | 100.0 |
| Column Total | 100.0 | | | |

$$x^2 = 0.0939$$

TABLE 4.7.

First Amendment Position and Attitude Toward
Closure for Non-Compliance with Sanitary Code.

| First Amendment Right to Free Expression | Per Cent | Compliance with the Sanitary Code | | Row Total |
|---|---|---|---|---|
| | | Agree | Disagree | |
| Group A YES | 49.7 | 77.4 | 22.7 | 100.1 |
| Group B NO | 50.3 | 92.1 | 7.9 | 100.0 |
| Column Total | 100.0 | | | |

$$x^2 = .0122$$

TABLE 4.8.

First Amendment Position and Attitude Toward
Closure Because of Services by Unlicensed Personnel.

| First Amendment Right to Free Expression | Per Cent | Service by Unlicensed Personnel | | Row Total |
| --- | --- | --- | --- | --- |
| | | Agree | Disagree | |
| Group A YES | 48.6 | 78.9 | 21.1 | 100.0 |
| Group B NO | 51.4 | 89.3 | 10.7 | 100.0 |
| Column Total | 100.0 | | | |

$$x^2 = .0777$$

and improbable cause for closure reflects a sensitivity to specious reasoning.

The last rationale for closure of adult entertainment establishments was "unlicensed personnel performing services". There was no significant difference between the two groups on this question. Both felt this was a legitimate reason for harassing these establishments. The question may arise as to what licensing is required for such enterprises which would exceed those in any other comparable business. The answer would be none if the businesses restricted themselves to films and books. However, many of the peepshow film outlets also offer "encounter" or "rap" sessions in the way of invitational activity suggested to the viewer/browser, which purport to be merely "massage" activity but in reality mask the fact of prostitution. Hence, the issues of basic licensing as well as the performance of unauthorized services arise.(1) (See Table 4.8.)

III.  THREE TYPICAL TIMES SQUARE ADULT ENTERTAIN-
      MENT BUSINESSES AND THEIR COMMUNITY IMPACT:
      Question 11

Three types of adult entertainment businesses were listed with accompanying visuals and the respondents were asked their opinion on how these businesses impacted on the neighborhood, in terms of legal and social implications. These were listed as follows:  (a) looks like a fire trap (b) brings jobs into the neighborhood (c) affects traffic conditions (d) contributes to changing venereal disease rates (e) whether these businesses had the right to operate (f) affects real estate values (g) attracts loiterers (h) need exists for these services (i) effect on crime rate in the neighborhood.(2)  All of these effects were tested on Group A, those agreeing with constitutional protection for operators of sex businesses, and Group B, those opposed to this protection.

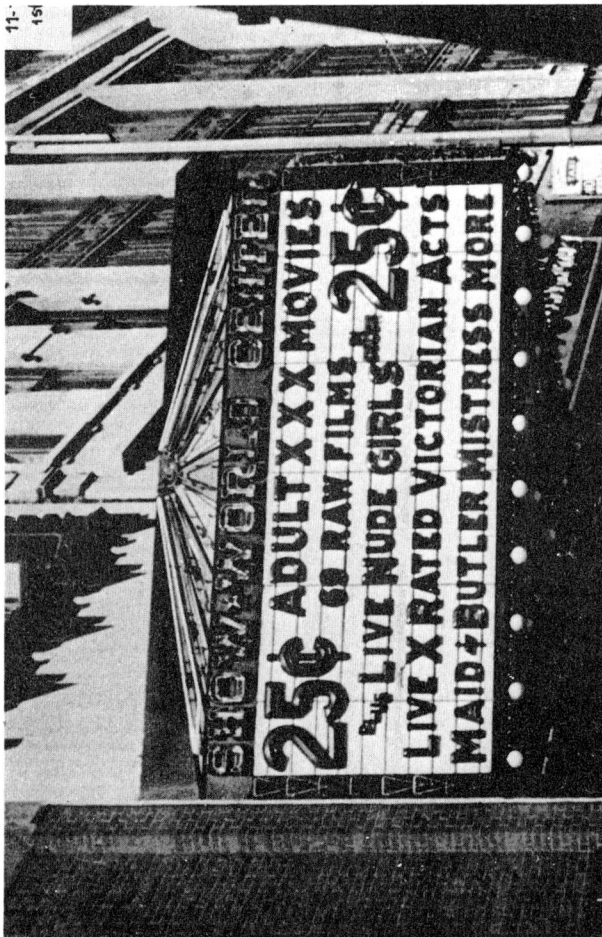

Photo One: Question 11, Column 1. Show World Center, located on the West side of Eighth Avenue between West 42 and West 43 Streets. April, 1977.
Photo: Lloyd Jenkins.

110

Photo Two: advertising for Show World Center.
April, 1977. Photo: Lloyd Jenkins.

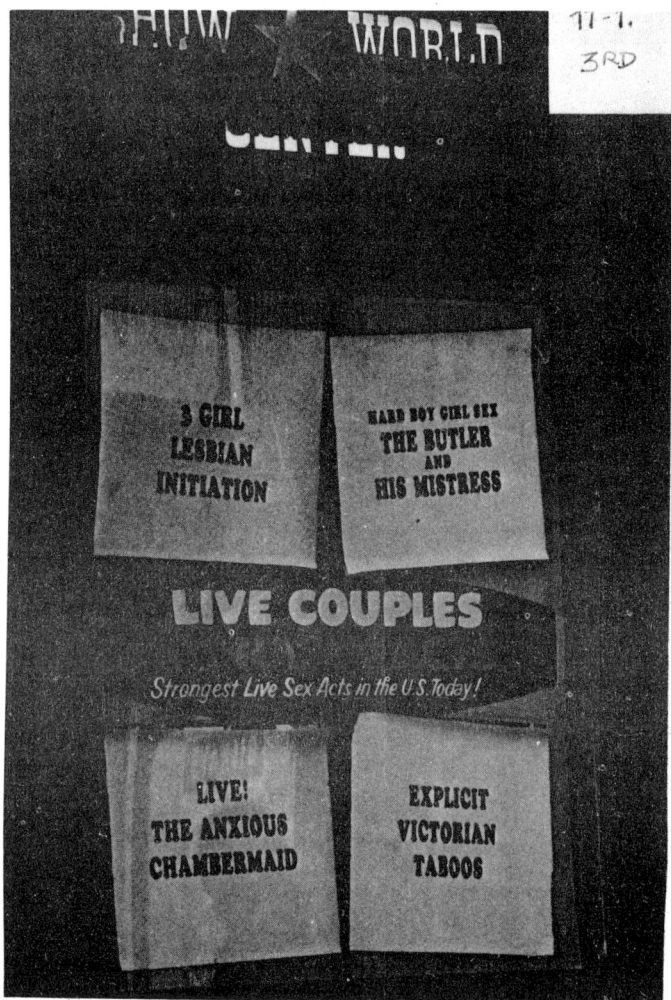

Photo Three: advertising for Show World Center.
April, 1977. Photo: Lloyd Jenkins.

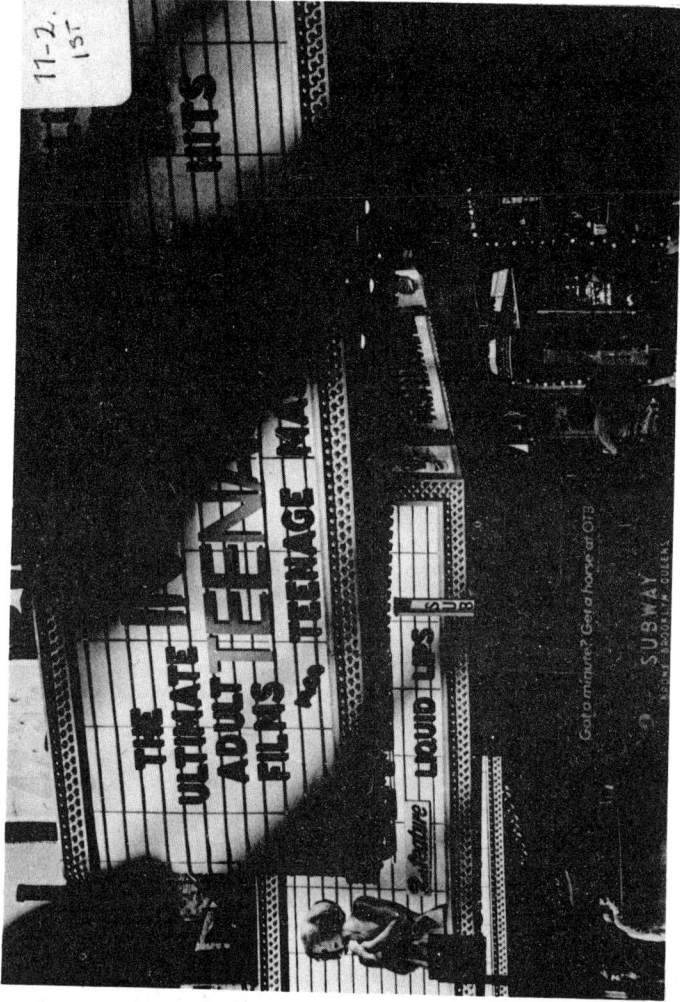

Photo Four: Question 11, Column 2. Cinema showing "Intimate Teenagers" Times Square, April, 1977.
Photo: Lloyd Jenkins

113

Photo Five: advertising for "Intimate Teenagers" April, 1977.
Photo: Lloyd Jenkins.

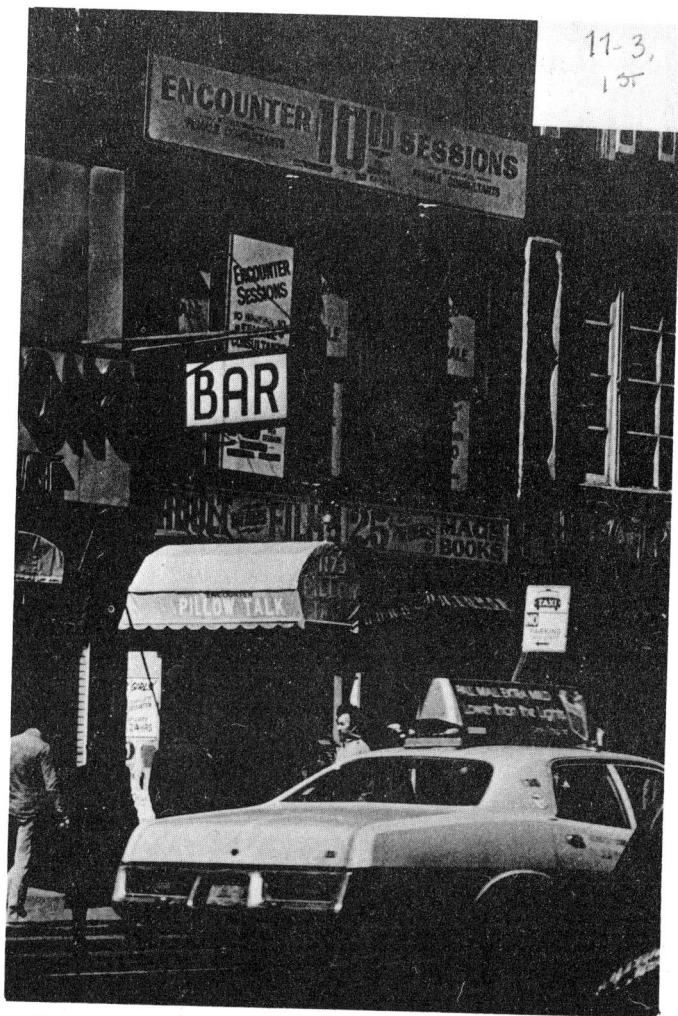

Photo Six: entrance to massage parlor located at
1173 Avenue of the Americas. April, 1977.
Photo: Lloyd Jenkins.

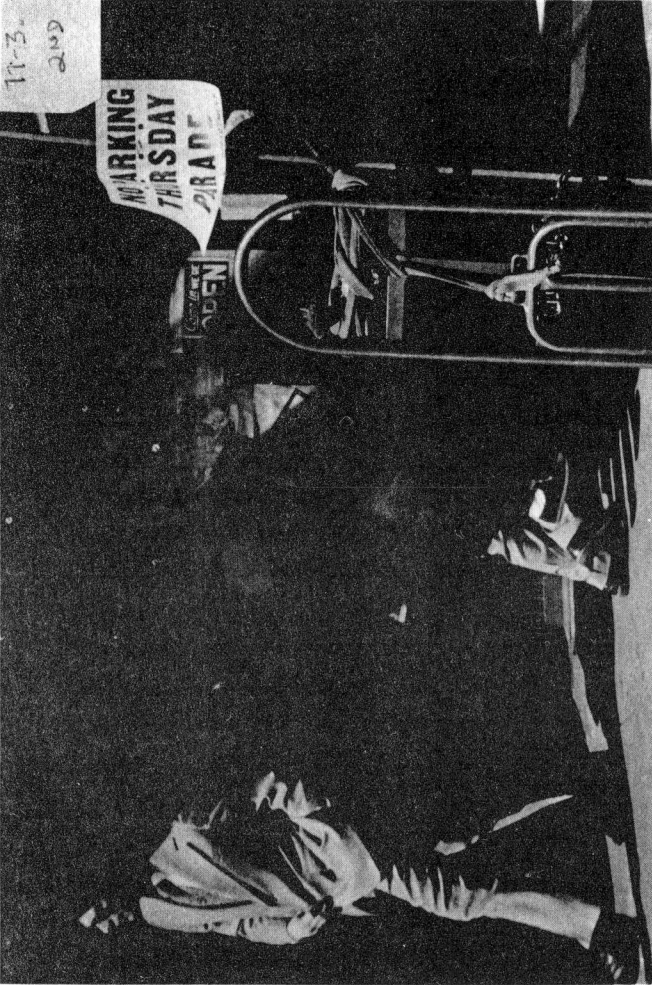

Photo Seven: window display and entrance to peep show. 1173 Avenue of the Americas, April, 1977. Photo: Lloyd Jenkins.

Both groups agreed that the live sex show, the film and the massage parlor were fire traps. There were no significant differences between the groups on the "fire trap" variable.(See Table 4.9.)

While no significant difference exists between Groups A and B in this question, the percentages reveal an increasing level of offensiveness as one moves from the live sex show to the massage parlor. This provides at least an informal appearance ranking based upon the visuals presented. Neither subjects nor interviewers were instructed with regard to the visuals except to display and study them in the order presented. The serendipity here lies in the subjects ranking as less offensive, even though a "fire trap" a converted legitimate movie house. While the movie house allegedly presented explicit x-rated performances, they are understated in terms of street level visuals, unlike the real state of the area where "Intimate Teenagers" is being exhibited, and least like the self-evident seediness of the massage parlor visuals. These subject perceptions indicate further the community's awareness of not just the adult displays and their contribution to an appearance of detertioration in the neighborhood.

The variable (b) "businesses bring jobs into the neighborhood" showed a significant difference between the two groups on the first two items - the show and the film. Group A which said these businesses had the right to operate, felt less strongly that these businesses did not bring jobs into the community. The difference in both cases was significant at the .05 level. (See Table 4.10.)

However, on the third section of Table 4.10, dealing with effect of massage parlors on neighborhood jobs, both Groups A and B felt that massage

## TABLE 4.9.

### First Amendment Attitude and Three Adult Entertainment Business Viewed as "Fire Traps".

### This Place Appears As A Fire Trap

| First Amendment Right to Free Expression | Per Cent | Live Sex Theatre "Show World" | | |
|---|---|---|---|---|
| | | Agree | Disagree | No Opinion |
| Group A  YES | 47.8 | 51.5 | 31.8 | 16.7 |
| Group B  NO | 52.2 | 59.7 | 29.2 | 11.1 |
| Column Total | 100.0 | | | |

$$x^2 = 0.5307$$

| First Amendment Right to Free Expression | Per Cent | Film: "Intimate Teenagers" | | |
|---|---|---|---|---|
| | | Agree | Disagree | No Opinion |
| Group A YES | 48.9 | 52.3 | 30.8 | 16.9 |
| Group B NO | 51.1 | 63.2 | 22.1 | 14.7 |
| Column Total | 100.0 | | | |

$$x^2 = 0.4175$$

| First Amendment Right to Free Expression | Per Cent | Massage Parlor | | |
|---|---|---|---|---|
| | | Agree | Disagree | No Opinion |
| Group A YES | 47.9 | 67.2 | 17.9 | 14.9 |
| Cropp B NO | 52.1 | 75.3 | 11.0 | 13.7 |
| Column Total | 100.0 | | | |

$$x^2 = 0.4617$$

## TABLE 4.10.

First Amendment Position and Attitude Toward Whether Businesses Bring More Jobs Into Neighborhood.

Business Brings Jobs Into The Neighborhood

| First Amendment Right to Free Expression | Per Cent | Live Sex Theatre "Show World" | | |
|---|---|---|---|---|
| | | Agree | Disagree | No Opinion |
| Group A YES | 50.0 | 27.4 | 71.2 | 1.4 |
| Group B NO | 50.0 | 8.2 | 89.0 | 2.7 |
| Column Total | 100.0 | | | |

$$x^2 = 0.0095$$

| First Amendment Right to Free Expression | Per Cent | Film: "Intimate Teenagers" | | |
|---|---|---|---|---|
| | | Agree | Disagree | No Opinion |
| Group A YES | 50.3 | 24.3 | 73.0 | 2.7 |
| Group B NO | 49.7 | 5.5 | 91.8 | 2.7 |
| Column Total | 100.0 | | | |

$$x^2 = 0.0050$$

| First Amendment Right to Free Expression | Per Cent | Massage Parlor | | |
|---|---|---|---|---|
| | | Agree | Disagree | No Opinion |
| Group A YES | 50.3 | 23.0 | 75.7 | 1.4 |
| Group B NO | 49.7 | 9.6 | 87.7 | 2.7 |
| Column Total | 100.0 | | | |

$$x^2 = 0.057$$

parlors had no positive effect in this respect on the community.

What is particularly difficult to adduce is the precise meaning of this statistic. It can be inferred that local people may be employed as ticket-takers in film houses, but the staffing of massage parlors is the province of people outside the community. This response is also consistent with the subjects' general negative attitude toward massage parlors in Question 11 a); and the relatively high offensiveness means in Questions 3 and 4 for activities associated with massage parlor operations.

. Respondents were asked next whether the existence of these three businesses had any discernible effect on the volume of traffic in the area, item 11 c). On the three variables, there was no significant difference between the two groups. Regardless of the groups' stand on the First Amendment question, they felt that these businesses did have an effect on traffic in the community. Both groups answered that these enterprises brought more traffic into the neighborhood. This finding is consistent with the survey data indicating that some of the businesses bring more jobs into the neighborhood as shown in Table 3.8.

The next factor examined was the perceived effect that these three establishments have on the level of venereal disease in the community. In considering this issue, both Groups A and B disagreed significantly that the presence of all three types of adult establishments in the area did bring a rise in the venereal disease rate. This disagreement was consistent with their respective stands on First Amendment Rights. (See Table 4.11.)

TABLE 4.11.

First Amendment Position and Belief that
Three Selected Sex Businesses Bring More
Venereal Disease Into Area.

Business Brings Venereal Disease Into Area

| First Amendment Right to Free Expression | Per Cent | Live Sex Theatre "Show World" | | |
| --- | --- | --- | --- | --- |
| | | Agree | Disagree | No Opinion |
| Group A  YES | 49.7 | 62.5 | 30.6 | 6.9 |
| Group B  NO | 50.3 | 89.0 | 8.2 | 2.7 |
| Column Total | 100.0 | | | |

$x^2 = .0009$

| First Amendment Right to Free Expression | Per Cent | Film: "Intimate Teenagers" | | |
| --- | --- | --- | --- | --- |
| | | Agree | Disagree | No Opinion |
| Group A  YES | 49.0 | 62.9 | 28.6 | 8.6 |
| Group B  NO | 51.0 | 83.6 | 12.3 | 4.1 |
| Column Total | 100.0 | | | |

$x^2 = .0196$

| First Amendment Right to Free Expression | Per Cent | Massage Parlor | | |
| --- | --- | --- | --- | --- |
| | | Agree | Disagree | No Opinion |
| Group A  YES | 48.3 | 74.3 | 17.1 | 8.6 |
| Group B  NO | 51.7 | 92.0 | 2.7 | 5.3 |
| Column Total | 100.0 | | | |

$x^2 = .0076$

121

The next question was a crucial one: 11 d)
did these establishments have the right to carry on
business where they were located? As could be
predicted, those who agree that these places are
protected by the First Amendment (Group A) also
agree that they have a right to do business where
they are.(See Table 4.12.)

The high level of statistical significance for
the first part of the table is related to the
"switch-over" per cent of First Amendment advocates
who chose to disagree with the right of a live
sex theatre to operate. The importance of this
control question cannot be overestimated. For the
71 respondents in Group A, when dealing with an
abstract principle, had no misgivings about its
applicabiltiy, yet when confronted with a specific
context in which it could be operative, 28 people,
or 39.4 per cent of Group A, altered their stand.

There is still a 59.2 per cent consistency on
the presumed First Amendment right. It can be
inferred that those who grant the entrepreneurs
the right to carry on business, are consistent in
their First Amendment attitude. The positions taken
on "Intimate Teenagers" and the massage parlor are
equally consistent with the ones relative to the
live sex show.

On the question of whether these three businesses
affect real estate values in item 11 f), respondents agree that they do affect property values in
the first two cases. However, on the matter of
whether the massage parlor affected real estate
values, the groups disagreed significantly at the
.04 level. Group B indicated that the massage parlor did, in fact, affect real estate values.

What is most significant in this data is the
near total agreement of philosophically opposing

TABLE 4.12.

First Amendment Position in the Abstract and in Context of Three Typical Times Square Adult Entertainment Businesses.

This Place Has A Right To Carry On Business Here

| First Amendment Right to Free Expression | Per Cent | Live Sex Theatre "Show World" | | |
|---|---|---|---|---|
| | | Agree | Disagree | No Opinion |
| Group A  YES | 49.3 | 59.2 | 39.4 | 1.4 |
| Group B  NO | 50.7 | 9.2 | 90.8 | - |
| Column Total | 100.0 | | | |

$$x^2 = .0000$$

| First Amendment Right to Free Expression | Per Cent | Film: "Intimate Teenagers" | | |
|---|---|---|---|---|
| | | Agree | Disagree | No Opinion |
| Group A  YES | 48.3 | 59.7 | 38.9 | 1.4 |
| Group B  NO | 51.7 | 7.9 | 90.8 | 1.3 |
| Column Total | 100.0 | | | |

$$x^2 = .0000$$

| First Amendment Right to Free Expression | Per Cent | Massage Parlor | | |
|---|---|---|---|---|
| | | Agree | Disagree | No Opinion |
| Group A  YES | 48.6 | 56.9 | 40.3 | 2.8 |
| Group B  NO | 51.4 | 9.2 | 89.5 | 1.3 |
| Column Total | 100.0 | | | |

$$x^2 = .0000$$

views. In previous analysis of Question 11, it was discerned that the manner in which real estate is affected by the adult entertainment industry is both positive and negative. A negative view is reenforced by local businessmen and property owners as they lobby for extensive urban renewal and a convention center which would help to displace the adult entertainment establishments. The campaign of Mr. Alex Parker, owner of the Allied Chemical Tower at 1 Times Square, involved turning off his new-relay light system for a period to dramatize the current effort at take-over of the area by pornographic entertainments. He also attempted to get 100,000 signatures of citizens decrying this same phenomenon. The campaign is representative of the concerned real estate groups for property values in the area. Legitimate theatre companies have also lobbied and publicly demonstrated their support for groups objecting to the adult entertainment industry's proximity to Broadway's legitimate theatres. However, it must be reiterated that some landlords have profited handsomely from the high rentals charged to adult entertainment tenants. A future study on the impact of "adult" businesses on the Clinton Times Square neighborhood might address itself more to gathering specific data on real estate values of the residential, commercial, industrial, and theatrical buildings in the area, and it would be interesting to know who are the owners of the various "adult" properties in question. (See Table 4.13.)

The next variable examined how respondents felt on the topic of loiterers in the neighborhood as related to these three types of adult entertainment. There was a significant difference between the two groups on whether they thought that the live sex show brought more of this activity into the community. Fewer of the Group A respondents feel that live sex shows bring loiterers into the area. However, both groups did agree that the other two

## TABLE 4.13.

First Amendment Position and Attitude on Whether
Massage Parlor Affects Real Estate Values.

| First Amendment Right to Free Expression | Per Cent | Massage Parlor Agree | Massage Parlor Disagree | No Opinion | Row Total |
|---|---|---|---|---|---|
| Group A  YES | 49.3 | 91.7 | 6.9 | 1.4 | 100.0 |
| Group B  NO | 50.7 | 100.0 | – | – | 100.0 |
| Column Total | 100.0 | | | | |

adult entertainment activities, the film "Intimate Teenagers" and the massage parlor, do bring more undesirables into the neighborhood. Even though Group A indicated that these two activities have the right to exist, they feel that as a result of their operations more "undesirable" persons come into the community. (See item 11 g), 2, 3, Appendix IV). (See Table 4.14.)

This table affirms a specific problem recognized by First Amendment advocates: namely, that there are detrimental effects to universal approbation of all forms of expression when examined in their concrete manifestations. While this table does not presume a shift in First Amendment attitutde by respondents, it does reveal their sensitivity to and candor on this issue.

The statement in item 11 h) "people want this service or it would not be there" brought a positive response, as both Groups A and B felt this to be the case but only for the live sex show and massage parlor. They disagree significantly on the relevance of the film.(See Table 4.15)

It is difficult to explain the particular objection to "Intimate Teenagers". However, the growing public concern over the use of children under 16 years of age in pornographic productions has been expressed on many occasions in the Clinton community and in Washington. (3) It is not unreasonable to infer some transfer effect to the survey population. This is also consistent with what was found by Kirkpatrick in the Midville study: that the designation of the problem by well-known public and community figures exacerbates the importance of the problem in the mind of the community.

Finally, item 11 i) asks: "do these adult entertainment activities have any effect on the

TABLE 4.14.

First Amendment Position and Attitude on Whether
Live Sex Theatre Attracts Undesirable Loiterers.

| First Amendment Right to Free Expression | Per Cent | Live Sex Theatre Attracts Undesirable Loiterers | | | Row Total |
| | | Agree | Disagree | No Opinion | |
|---|---|---|---|---|---|
| Group A  YES | 49.0 | 91.8 | 8.2 | 0.0 | 100.0 |
| Group B  NO | 51.0 | 98.7 | 0.0 | 1.3 | 100.0 |
| Column Total | 100.0 | | | | |

$$x^2 = .0248$$

TABLE 4.15.

First Amendment Position and Attitude
Toward Presence of Service.

| First Amendment Right to Free Expression | Per Cent | "Intimate Teenagers" - People want This Service Or It Would Not Be There | | | |
|---|---|---|---|---|---|
| | | Agree | Disagree | No Opinion | Row Total |
| Group A  YES | 49.3 | 63.0 | 34.2 | 2.7 | 99.9 |
| Group B  NO | 50.7 | 42.7 | 56.0 | 1.3 | 100.0 |
| Column Total | 100.0 | | | | |

$$x^2 = .0282$$

128

crime rate in the community?" Both Groups A and B feel that the massage parlor has an effect on the area crime rate. This bears some examination in light of item 11 b) pertaining to jobs. It is not certain whether the respondents perceive the massage parlor as a locus for organized crime activities or as criminogenic itself. It is known that patrons of massage parlors are often robbed of wallets, keys, cash, credit cards and that these losses are more apt to be reported to police than patronizing a massage parlor; i.e., a house of prostitution. (See Table 4.16.)

Both Groups A and B did disagree on the contributing aspects to crime of the live sex show and film house. The respondents, and Group A in particular, hold that these do not have as dramatic an effect on the crime rate. Group B was consistent with its First Amendment stand: it felt that these places do bring more crime into the neighborhood.

From the analysis just presented of Question 11, it can be said that Group B, tends to blame all of the community ills listed in the question on the presence of adult entertainment activities. On the other hand, Group A feels that some adult entertainments do appear to be fire traps. If this is borne in mind, one rationale for the closing of any of these businesses could be based on the presumption that they are a fire hazard. Question 8 c) demonstrates that civil libertarians accepted police harassment for closure on grounds of fire hazard. If these two approaches are related, it becomes clear that for Group A to agree to close a business, a clear and present danger to the safety of the customers must be demonstrated.

Question 16 asked: "How would you vote for the following proposals?"

TABLE 4.16.

First Amendment Position and Attitude on Whether A Sex Business Brings More Crime Into the Neighborhood.

This Place Brings More Crime Into The Neighborhood

Live Sex Theatre "Show World"

| First Amendment Right to Free Expression | Per Cent | Agree | Disagree | No Opinion |
|---|---|---|---|---|
| Group A YES | 49.0 | 82.2 | 16.4 | 1.4 |
| Group B NO | 51.0 | 94.7 | 3.9 | 1.3 |
| Column Total | 100.0 | | | |

$$x^2 = .0401$$

"Intimate Teenagers" - Film

| First Amendment Right to Free Expression | Per Cent | Agree | Disagree | No Opinion |
|---|---|---|---|---|
| Group A YES | 49.0 | 83.6 | 13.7 | 2.7 |
| Group B NO | 51.0 | 96.1 | 2.6 | 1.3 |
| Column Total | 100.0 | | | |

$$x^2 = .0354$$

Massage Parlor

| First Amendment Right to Free Expression | Per Cent | Agree | Disagree | No Opinion |
|---|---|---|---|---|
| Group A YES | 49.3 | 87.8 | 10.8 | 1.4 |
| Group B NO | 50.7 | 93.4 | 3.9 | 2.6 |
| Column Total | 100.0 | | | |

$$x^2 = .2412$$

130

TABLE 4.17.

Response of the Two Groups to the First Proposal.

a. Present City Planning Commission Proposal forbidding location of
   adult entertainment within 500 feet of a residential district.

| First Amendment Right to Free Expression | Per Cent | Agree | Disagree | No Opinion |
|---|---|---|---|---|
| Group A  YES | 48.6 | 80.6 | 16.7 | 2.8 |
| Group B  NO | 51.4 | 71.1 | 27.6 | 1.3 |
| Column Total | 100.0 | | | |

x = 0.139

TABLE 4.18.

Response of the Two Groups to the Second Proposal

b. Decriminalize Prostitution (make it not punishable under the criminal code).

| First Amendment Right to Free Expression | Per Cent | Agree | Disagree | Row Total |
|---|---|---|---|---|
| Group A  YES | 49.3 | 69.4 | 30.6 | 100.0 |
| Group B  NO | 50.7 | 45.9 | 54.1 | 100.0 |
| Column Total | 100.0 | | | |

$$x^2 = 0.0068$$

TABLE 4.19.

Response of the Two Troups to the Third Proposal.

c. Legalize All Adult Entertainment Business.

| First Amendment Right to Free Expression | Per Cent | Agree | Disagree | No Opinion | Row Total |
|---|---|---|---|---|---|
| Group A   YES | 48.3 | 62.3 | 36.2 | 1.4 | 99.9 |
| Group B   NO | 51.7 | 36.5 | 63.5 | – | 100.0 |
| Column Total | 100.0 | | | | |

$$x^2 = 0.0037$$

Neither group is opposed to this proposal.
However, a higher percentage of Group B respondents disagreed with the plan. There was no significant difference between the two groups when responding to the plan: "restricting the number of adult establishments within each zoning area". Both groups are in favor of abating somewhat the intensity of the sex businesses: 75.3 per cent of Group A, and 69.7 per cent of Group B were in agreement with the proposal.

Difference was insignificant also in the case of the statement on "a zoning law which would place all adult entertainment businesses in only one, non-residential part of the city". 81.9 per cent of Group A were in favor of this idea; as were 79.7 per cent of Group B respondents. Significant differences exist between the two groups regarding the last two proposals on the trial ballot.

Group A is much more in favor of decriminalization than the others. All respondents who answered the question expressed a definite opinion: there were no undecided answers.

In the matter of the final proposal offered the respondents, tabulated above, Group B did not think this activity should receive legal sanctions. (See Table 4.19.)

IV.  SUMMARY

General Attitude Toward Sex Entertainments.
Question 5 tested the liberality or severity of respondents toward sexually-oriented entertainments of a private nature, experienced only by a willing audience and with no perceptible street impact. The question took the form of describing filmed sexual activities and asked whether the respondent

felt this should be allowed for viewing. Of six activities, the only one which 50 per cent of respondents deemed allowable was a scene showing male or female genitalia. Overall, the response to this question can be considered a conservative one regarding the appropriateness of filmed sex scenes in a private viewing context, aimed presumably at a willing audience.

First Amendment Position and Attitude Toward Times Square Pornography. The consistency of First Amendment position as measured in answers to the first question was tested by cross-tablulation with the survey population's responses to specific activities which may be covered by the protections of the Amendment, but which may also be pornographic or obscene. In terms of simple percentages, the respondents were almost evenly divided in the response to the first question, which asked whether they felt operators of adult businesses were protected in this activity by the First Amendment. The presentation of this as the initial question prevented a cumulative effect on the respondent as he or she was asked more detailed questions later in the interview. The generally balanced position taken by the respondents on the whole issue is to be noted. While they later revealed themselves to be a group highly offended by certain aspects of the sex businesses, they were willing to tolerate much of the activity as long as it was not thrust upon them as "unwilling audience." Hence the comment most often recorded in support of the industry's self-expression was "Yes, it is permissible if it does not infringe on my rights". Conversely, those who opposed such self-expression most often gave the comment"...it violates other rights." Taken on the whole, it can be affirmed that respondents are able to appreciate the nature of the conflict between rights of expression and

and rights of privacy. Responses to the question on the First Amendment (Question 1) were cross-tabulated with answers to the question on filmed sex scenes (Question 5), and submitted to statistical analysis. The only filmed sex scene which a majority of First Amendment proponents found acceptable was the one showing male and female genitalia. Five other sexual activities described in Question 5 did not receive majority approval of the "liberal" element in the population as fit subjects for private viewing. For those sampled who were opposed to First Amendment protections for pornographers, every item was disapproved of by a majority of respondents. The attitude of the latter group is predictable. It is the response pattern of those with a liberal position that demonstrates the conservative nature of the respondents. The overall negative response regarding whether filmed sex scenes should be allowed is better understood when one considers the high mean offensiveness ratings given by all respondents in other questions associated with prostitution activities, live sex shows, and massage parlors:  all of which involve personal interaction.

Another question which was cross-tabulated with the First Amendment responses was one asking how respondents would feel if law enforcement officers harassed bookstores or film theatres by closing them down on grounds other than obscenity. When asked how they reacted to closing of these businesses on grounds of false advertising, both groups felt that this was a legitimate reason for closing these places, as such advertising does violate the Administrative Code of the City. There was significant difference between the two groups on the next option for closure:  lack of air space. Those who felt that the right to operate this enterprise was protected by our Constitution were not going to accept lack of air space as a legitimate reason for closure. The next rationale that was offered for closure of businesses was violation of fire code. As no significant difference came through in the responses of both groups, it must be concluded that First Amendment position did not operate in this circumstance, probably bacause noncompliance with the fire code implies an immediate danger to life. When the reason for closing an x-rated film or bookstore was "inadequate sanitary facilities", the two groups again significantly differed according to their characteristic First Amendment position. It is noteworthy that respondents display a certain sophistication in discerning probable and improbable cause for closure of sex businesses; while the specifics of false advertising and noncompliance with the fire code are demonstrable by administrative law, the health regulations are less precise in this area.

The question which was analyzed for offensiveness was also submitted for analysis against respondents' First Amendment position. Photographs of the fronts of a live sex show, adult film and a massage parlor accompanied ten statements made about each of the establishments. Respondents were asked to agree or disagree with the statements: A) looks like a fire trap b) brings business into the neighborhood c) affects traffic conditions d) contributes to changing venereal disease rates e) whether the business in the photo had a right to operate f) the business affected real estate values g) attract loiterers h) need exists for these services i) effect on neighborhood crime rate.

There was no significant difference between the two groups holding opposing views on the First Amendment regarding the fire trap variable: both groups agreed that all three establishments were fire traps. Regarding b): bringing in more jobs, there was a significant difference between the two groups on the live show and the film; however, the respondents did not differ regarding the massage parlor, saying in effect that it had no positive effect on community jobs.

Analysis of the next two statements revealed that both groups believed that the presence of the three adult businesses in their midst resulted in an increased volume of traffic and a rise in the v.d. rate. The stated First Amendment position of respondents, when placed against their replies concerning whether the three places in question had a right to be where they were, was highly significant. Of seventy-one respondents who had replied "Yes" to the constitutional question, 28 of them, or 39.4 per cent altered their stand on the live sex show. The positions taken on the adult film and massage parlor are equally consistent regarding a "switchover" from tolerance of their presence in Question 1, to disapproval of their presence in this question.

Respondents of both groupings agreed that property values were affected in the case of the x-rated film house and the live sex show. However, on the massage parlor's effect, there was disagreement between the two groups, with those opposed to First Amendment protection giving 100 per cent agreement to the statement that the massage parlor did in fact affect real estate values. As was mentioned in the discussion of general responses of all those surveyed on this question, the analysis showed that it is thought sex businesses both positively and negatively affect real estate values. The negative view is reinforced by local businessmen and property owners as they lobby for extensive urban renewal in the area, and a convention center on 44th Street, which would help to displace adult entertainment establishments. On the other hand, some landlords have profited handsomely from the high rentals charged to tenants purveying x-rated entertainments. Future studies on the impact of "adult" businesses on the Clinton-Times Square area might address themselves more to gathering specific data on the history of fluctuating real estate market value of the residential, commercial, industrial, and theatrical buildings in the neighborhood. It would also be of interest to research ownership patterns of the various adult properties in question.

When examined on whether they felt undesirable loiterers were attracted by these three places, respondents differed significantly regarding the live sex show: with fewer of First Amendment proponents agreeing to the statement. However, both groups were united in agreeing to the statement regarding loiterers drawn by the film and the massage parlor. The statement "People want this service or it would not be there" brought a positive response from both groups in the cases of the live sex show and the massage parlor; for the film theatre, there was significant disagreement on the statement from the group opposed to First Amendment protections. This particular objection might be explained by the fact that in 1977, there was widely publicized public concern in the area over the growing use of children under 17 years of age in pornographic productions. It is not unreasonable to infer some transfer effect to the survey population.

The final item in the question asks whether these adult entertainment businesses have any effect on the crime rate in the community. Both groups do feel that the massage parlor has an effect on the area's crime rate. As for the contributing aspects of the sex show and film house, the groups were in disagreement: in particular, the group adhering to First Amendment protections held that these do not affect the crime rate as much; the other group was consistent with its constitutional stand: it felt that these places do bring more crime into the neighborhood.

In summing up the analysis of the two groups, each with a differing position on First Amendment rights, against their attitudes toward sexually-oriented entertainment for private viewing, it must be concluded that both groups were equally conservative in what they might allow to be exhibited in a film. When presented with reasons for harassing adult entertainment places to close down, the two groups were united in agreeing that fire hazard was a legitimate ground for closing sex businesses. Again, when they considered the photographs of the three typical adult businesses, respondents were willing to label all three as representative of fire hazard. It can therefore be inferred that for those who were liberal on constitutional protection for pornography, a clear and present danger to the safety of customers must be demonstrated before they would agree to close a business. Both groups disagreed with the statement that all three businesses had a right to be where they were; but agreed to the statements that these enterprises brought more traffic and venereal disease into the area.

# FOOTNOTES

1.  People v. 1173 Avenue of the Americas Corp.

2.  In the matter of (d) venereal disease and (i)
    crime rate, see Chapter III.  The particular
    difficulty of assessing the accuracy of any
    data is complexified by the variegated reporting
    systems and demographic divisions employed
    by health and police agencies.

3.  N.Y. Times 7/1/77

CHAPTER V

IMAGES, ENTERTAINMENT AND
THE INDUSTRY

Question 9 represents an attempt to encourage respondents to sift in their minds what precise elements they find acceptable or unacceptable in sexually oriented stage entertainments. The play O Calcutta was chosen as an example because it was one of the first "sexual musicals" prominently advertised as a Broadway offering. It also has certain stage resemblances to a live sex show – subject matter, nudity, and dancing on stage to music. The statement that both contain sexual activity on stage might be forcing the comparison. However, this was justified by the fact that the format of the question is somewhat hypothetical, and enabled the investigators to observe attitudinal processes in motion.

The question states that both offerings contain nudity and sexual activity on stage, and asks which they think the City would have reason to close. Table 5.1 contains the spread of opinion in the responses. The category "Both" was added by the researchers while tabulating the questionnaire responses.

Question 10 asks "Why do you think that?" in an attempt to get a rationale for the respondent's choice on Question 9. More than half of the 42.3 percent who responded that the live sex show should be closed used O Calcutta as the criteria for closing it, and not the sex show itself. O Calcutta was mentioned in 40 of the responses dealing with the live sex show. Below is a tabulation made of thevocabulary used in responses to Question 10. (Table 5.2) The words used for O Calcutta construct a defense for the legitimacy of this production, while those used for the sex show are more deprecating and associated with deviance in entertainment quality. Quantitative lexical analysis of the"live sex show" responses provided a graphic illustration of how the sex show compares with a Broadway offering in the minds of the respondents. (Table 5.3.)

TABLE 5.1.

Respondents' Opinions on Which Of Two Shows
The City Might Find Reason to Close.

| O Calcutta | Live Sex Show | Neither | Don't Know | Both |
|---|---|---|---|---|
| 3.4 | 42.3 | 20.8 | 6.7 | 26.8 |

**TABLE 5.2.**

Vocabulary Used by Respondents to Refer to Both
Shows in Replying "The City Would Close the Live
Sex Show"

| "O CALCUTTA" USED IN REPLY | SEX SHOW USED IN REPLY |
|---|---|
| it's entertaining | It's not entertaining |
| an organized production | a disorganized production |
| draws a different crowd | riffraff go to see it |
| it's theatre | it's obscene |
| it's legitimate | just smut |
| has artistic value | sleazy |
| it's entertainment | no staging; less taste |
| humorous toward sex | has explicit sex acts |
| there's comedy, dancing | hard-core porn |
| has a story line | no artistic "merit" |
| more respectful | appeals to "prurient interest" |
| doesn't affect my way of | patently offensive |
| living as aggressively | exploits sex |
| not evil | vulgar by design |
| advertising not offensive | more exciting |
| I give it the benefit of | |
| the doubt | |

| OTHER REASONS FOR CLOSING "O CALCUTTA" | OTHER REASONS FOR CLOSING LIVE SEX SHOW |
|---|---|
| Just in one place | all over the place; a nuisance to the community |
| has more money back of it more | actors just out to make a buck |
| solid citizens back of it | Mayor Beame closed one. down |

TABLE 5.3.

Views of Theatre Offerings

| COMMENT | No. of TIMES MENTIONED |
|---|---|
| O Calcutta is entertaining | 8 |
| "    "    is legitimate | 17 |
| "    "    has artistic value | 10 |
| Sex Show is pornography | 16 |

Comments given by those respondents who indicated that O Calcutta would be closed by the City were: 1) offensive advertising 2) easier to close one show that the numerous live sex shows which are more difficult to control 3) artists should know better than street people. The final comment indicates that the respondent felt O Calcutta should close because this person associates legitimacy with a Broadway production, and therefore attributes to the show a greater sense of social responsibility regarding public sexual expression.

Reasons given by the 6.7 per cent of the respondents who answered "Don't Know" to Question 10 follow. These remarks show that some interviewees are not willing to hazard a reply without having experienced either show. One is conscious of a shift in attitude on their part regarding First Amendment principles; while the respondent who is puzzled that prostitution apparently is being sanctioned seems to be saying: "Why close representations of sexual activity when the real thing is allowed to exist on the streets of Times Square?" (See Table 5.4.)

Those who indicated that neither show should be closed made up 20.8 per cent of the respondents. The reasons are given in Table 5.5.

Taken as a whole, these replies are testimony that a significant portion of respondents believe that a "willing audience" does exist for entertainment which may be pornographic, and that under our Constitution this audience has a right to see whatever it wishes. One qualification made, however, is that there be no offensive street advertising for these shows. An analysis of the principal terminology used by the respondents with the most liberal attitude follows in Table 5.6.

TABLE 5.4.

Respondents Views

1. I've not seen either;

2. I can't be fair at this point on the First Amendment;

3. Don't know the law;

4. Not much difference between allowing sex shows to exist and allowing prostitution;

TABLE 5.5.

Respondents Replies to Show Closing.

1. government shouldn't get involved in questions of taste;
2. who's to say what is legitimate?
3. O Calcutta was considered trash 10 years ago;
4. it's our attitude toward sexuality which is bad;
5. both are theatrical presentations;
6. you can easily avoid them both;
7. if one pays for these, o.k.;
8. all are performers;
9. persons have a right to see what they wish;
10. both are entertainment in "legal" places;
11. neither are offensive;
12. as long as there's no offensive street advertising or leafletting;
13. o.k. until Supreme Court can define obscenity;
14. both are off the street.

TABLE 5.6.

The Willing Audience

| COMMENT | No. of TIMES MENTIONED |
|---|---|
| They are private offerings | 6 |
| not a matter for governmental regulation | 3 |
| both are legitimate entertainment | 5 |

Whether this information translates into an interest in pornography _per se_ on the part of these respondents, or merely a recognition of freedom to engage in such activity is not clear.

26.8 per cent of respondents indicated that both shows should be closed, for the following reasons. Since these respondents were replying to a category not previously provided by the questionnaire, it is inferred that they did not agree with any attempt to distinguish between the two shows, but preferred to condemn both shows. Vocabulary tends to be categorical and some rely on traditional moral or religious concepts to bolster their judgments. The analysis of principal terminology used by respondents with the most severe attitude follows in Table 5.7.

While 72.5 per cent of the respondents thought the City would close at least one show, the reasons given for their choice reflect a lack of consensus about what constitutes "offensiveness" in public advertising for the two shows. Advertising for O Calcutta is seen as not offensive in rationales used to indicate the City would close the sex show; it appears as offensive when used as a reason to close O Calcutta and in responses indicating that both shows should be closed.(See Table 5.8.)

Further analysis of Question 9 consisted in comparing the five categories of replies to attitudes toward the First Amendment as shown in Question 1. Those who agreed to First Amendment protection for sex businesses would be expected to have a more liberal view of closing shows; those who disagreed that the First Amendment protects operators of pornographic entertainments would be expected to be more severe in their replies.(See Table 5.9.)

TABLE 5.7.

Rationale For Closings

1. both shows are:   obscene material
                     the same thing
                     bad
                     offensive
                     indecent
                     a disgrace
                     vulgar - pornography
                     use nudity to sell a show
                     corrupt people
                     morally wrong

2. there's a time and place for sex - not on stage;
3. why ban a show on 8th Ave. or 42nd St. and not Broadway;
4. O Calcutta not legitimate, either;
5. if we start making distinctions, then we'll get more and more
      of these shows;
6. I resent O Calcutta advertising photos;
7. the Bible says "nakedness should not be seen".

152

TABLE 5.8.

Terminology For Closing

| COMMENT | No. of TIMES MENTIONED |
|---|---|
| sex should not be public | 7 |
| both are obscene | 3 |
| both are immoral | 3 |
| both are offensive | 15 |

TABLE 5.9

First Amendment Position and Attitude on Closing
Theatrical Presentation.

| 1st Amendment Right to Free Expression | Percent | O Calcutta | Live Sex Show | Neither | Don't Know | Both | Row Total |
|---|---|---|---|---|---|---|---|
| Group A  YES | 48.6 | 2.8 | 40.8 | 36.6 | 2.8 | 16.9 | 99.9 |
| Group B  NO | 51.4 | 4.0 | 42.7 | 5.3 | 10.7 | 37.3 | 100.0 |
| Column Total | 100.0 | | | | | | |

$$x^2 = .0000$$

There was a significant difference between
the two groups. 43.6 per cent of those agreeing
with First Amendment principles would close at
least one show, while 46.7 per cent of those dis-
agreeing with the protections afforded by the Amendment would close one show. However, 36.6 percent
of the "liberals" regarding the First Amendment
felt that neither of the shows should be banned;
and only 16.9 per cent felt that both should be
closed. On the other hand, 5.3 per cent of the
"conservatives" felt that neither performance should
be shut down, and 37.3 per cent of this group felt
that both should be closed.

The respondents' use of words like "legitimate"
and "offensive" when referring to the two shows
amounts to a belief that there should exist
definite boundaries of propriety where sex entertainments are concerned. The terms "prurient
interest" and "patently offensive" are the exact
words used for some elements required for material
to be obscene in the text of the 1973 Miller
decision. In many cases, Broadway, O Calcutta
and legitimacy were equated; a few mentioned 8th
Avenue as the locus of illicit entertainments such
as the sex shows. This may seem like a logical
geographic view of things but any Clinton resident
knows that for all purposes, the two streets are
in the same neighborhood. While there are no
major playhouses on 8th Avenue, many adult movie
houses and peep shows are now to be found on
Broadway.

The question of concentration and permanence
of the nuisance which were brought up in comments
on Question 3 and 7 also comes through in comments
where live sex shows are seen to be numerous:
"they are all over the place; therefore, a nuisance
to the community" so that "they affect my way of
living", while O Calcutta is not perceived as such
a threat to one's lifestyle.

Summary

Question 9 asked the respondent to choose
whether a "sexual" musical like O Calcutta or a
live sex show would be the first to be closed by
the City. The question represents an attempt on
the part of the researchers to discern what elements respondents find acceptable or unacceptable
in sexually-oriented stage entertainments. In
tabulating the responses, the category "Both"
was added to the replies. 3.4 per cent would have
the City close "O Calcutta"; 42.3 per cent the
live sex show; 20.8 said "Neither"; 26.8 per cent
said "Both"; 6.7 per cent did not know. Question
10 asked "Why do You think that?" The responses
to this open-ended question lent themselves to
lexical analysis regarding expressions used to
refer to both shows. The words used for O Calcutta
construct a defense for the legitimacy of this production; in addition, it is identified with
Broadway offerings. Analysis of vocabulary used
in responses about the live sex show provides a
graphic illustration of the deviance associated
with these productions. It follows from the two
foregoing identifications, one with legitimacy
and the other with deviance, that "art", "good
people", "artistic value", "money back of it",
"entertainment", are words used to describe
"O Calcutta"; while "smut", "sleazy", "hard-core
porn", "prurient", "exploitative", "riffraff",
are words employed to describe the live sex show.

It is noteworthy to mention here that those
who did not want either show closed, or 20.8 per
cent of respondents, believed that a "willing
audience" does exist for entertainment which may
be pornographic, and that under our Constitution
this audience has a right to see whatever it wishes.
One qualification made by this segment of respondents,

however, is that there be no offensive street
advertising for these shows. Whether this translates into an interest in pornography _per se_
on the part of these subjects, or merely a
recognition of freedom to engage in such activity,
is not clear.

CHAPTER VI

THE LEGISLATIVE/ENFORCEMENT REMEDY

The purpose of a study of this kind should include decision-making options or suggested avenues of action which are available to the population. Question sixteen presented to the respondent five choices of action. The first two proposals are taken from the most recent zoning plan proposed by the New York City Planning Commission and subjected to various public hearings during the Spring of 1977.(1) All of the proposals in this question have been suggested and/or implemented in other cities and states.

Table 6.1 ranks the respondent's choices to Question 16 in order of preferred regulation. In replying to Question 16, the sample of voters preferred item b): 81.2 per cent would vote "yes" to a proposal which would place all adult entertainment businesses in one, non-residential part of the city. Consistent with their choices in Question 11 e) and h), they are prepared to accept an adult entertainment/red light district like Hamburg, Germany or downtown Boston, as long as it is isolated from the residential pooulation. Questionnaires show ten recorded comments relating to Question 16 b). Six of them indicated that the adult entertainment trade should be relegated to another part of the city or outside it. Eight of the fourteen comments recorded on questionnaires for 16 c) and d), whether answered positively or negatively, indicated that legalization of prostitution and all places of adult entertainment should involve removing it from the neighborhood context.

It will be recalled that high mean offensiveness ratings were given to the aspects of sex entertainments which are visible to the respondents. Should it not be feasible to isolate the commercial sex industry from residential neighborhoods, then

TABLE 6.1.

Preferred Ranking for Lawful Regulation of Adult Entertainment.

| TYPE OF REGULATION | % Yes | % No | % No Opinion | Row Total |
|---|---|---|---|---|
| 1) A zoning law which would place all adult entertainment businesses in only one, non-residential part of the city | 81.2 | 18.1 | 0.7 | 100 |
| 2) The present City Planning Commission proposals: a) forbidding location of adult entertainments within 500' of a residential district | 75.5 | 22.5 | 1.3 | 99.3 |
| b) restricting the number of adult entertainments within each zoning are | 73.0 | 24.3 | 2.6 | 99.9 |
| 3) Decriminalize prostitution (make it not punishable under the criminal code) | 57.7 | 42.3 | 0 | 100 |
| 4) Legalize all adult entertainments | 48.6 | 50.7 | 0.7 | 100 |

respondents would accept zoning restrictions which
would regulate the growth of these businesses as
described in Questions 16, 2a) and 2b). While more
favor decriminalization of prostitution than not,
the support for this position is neither clearcut
nor overwhelming. The least acceptable proposal,
to "legalize all adult entertainment businesses"
posesa dilemma insofar as it implicitly contradicts
option number one, if one accepts legalization as
meaning the "status quo". It is clear that respondents favor permissibility for the adult entertainment industry, recognizing that it meets needs
of a segment of the population but wish the locale
for the provision of the services to be sufficiently
removed from a community context to prevent its
functioning to the detriment of the residential
population.

I.  PROSTITUTION AND THE RESTRICTION OF PUBLIC
    CONDUCT

     According to the Supreme Court justices, when
behavior is involved, a different question is
presented regarding First Amendment protections.
The situation must be analyzed to determine which
element: action or expression, can be said to
dominate. The First Amendment, then, does not
restrict the control of conduct; indeed this is
the primary business of the government. (2)

     As indicated in the police records - both
those presented and those not possible to record in
this study, there is widespread prostitution in
Times Square which spills over into the Clinton
neighborhood. There are certain elements of
prostitution operations which have become a problem
for the respondents in this survey, and which
involve behavior rather than expression.

Question 4 gave respondents the opportunity to express the degree to which they were offended by any one particular activity of adult entertainment. It must be reiterated here that highest offensiveness ratings possible, "9", were accorded actions associated with prostitution by those who answered Question 4. An illustration of this point is made in Table 6.2 of those items whose means were above the overall mean.

The carrying on of female prostitution in public streets is the activity most offensive to the survey population. The question of street prostitution in the area of a homosexual and transvestite nature was included only peripherally, if only because it was intended to present respondents with as complete a picture as possible of activities which do exist in their neighborhood streets. It was realized during the interviewing phase that while transvestites do solicit publicly, especially on Tenth Avenue near the entrance to the Lincoln Tunnel, homosexual prostitutes do not walk the streets - they prefer to gather in specific bars or theatres of Times Square. The lack of visibility of this activity may account for the fact that Question 4 h): "homosexual pickups in the area" received the lowest offensiveness rating: 6.40. On the other hand, Question 4 i): "transvestite solicitation on Tenth Avenue" which is as garish an activity as it is visible, received a 7.5 rating on the offensiveness scale.

Second highest offensiveness rating in Question 4 went to item c): "men standing outside massage parlors calling out availability of women inside". This activity might be construed as "pimping."

TABLE 6.2

Offensiveness of Street Activity

| TYPES OF STREET ACTIVITY | Mean Offensiveness Score |
|---|---|
| Question 4 b) solicitation by prostitutes in streets | 8.152 |
| c) men standing outside massage parlors calling out availability of women inside | 7.993 |
| d) photos at entrances of massage parlors emphasizing female sexual anatomy | 7.664 |
| f) noise connected with prostitution and activities at night on street, in parking or empty lots | 7.986 |

Overall Mean Score = 7.541

The mean offensiveness for leafletting as described in item 1) of this question was below the overall mean of 7.5. Passing out a printed leaflet about massage parlor women could be legally construed as engaging in a protected expression, while calling out about the same becomes less clearly "expression" because the mode of behavior involved in it is seen as quite offensive. Street leaf-letters do not always restrict themselves to pass-ing out their wares in silence. They sometimes encourage acceptance of their wares by calling out "Check it out!" However, when this neutral remark becomes "Baby, I'd like to check you out!" addressed loudly to women passersby who are not offered the leaflet in question, then it is easier to trace the shift from protected expression to action or behavior which is offensive. On this basis, there is ground for legislative remedy for such situations, which presently exist.

In Question 11, over 80 percent of respondents agreed that massage parlors brought crime and venereal disease into the area, reinforcing the negative image given by these establishments.

Question 17 offers specific remedies for some of the issues which constitute the nuisance factors. It was explained to the respondents that they could indicate more than one option for each problem presented in the adult entertainment industry. Of the six possible options, three were chosen more than four hundred fifty (450) times. These were: Remedy 5: Pass legislation totally forbidding this chosen 556 times; Remedy 4: Police should enforce existing laws chosen 503 times; Remedy 1: Pass legislation to keep off the streets chosen 472 times. The other three options were chosen less often. These remedy options appear in the graphs which follow on pages 168, 169 and 170.

164

TABLE 6.3.

Frequency Distribution of Remedy
by Activity Relationship.

| Adult Entertainment Activity | Remedy Number | | | | | |
|---|---|---|---|---|---|---|
| **Part I** **Direct Relationship** | 1 | 2 | 3 | 4 | 5 | 6 |
| a. men "leafletting" for massage parlors | 64 | | | | | |
| b. solicitation by prostitutes | 69 | | | | | |
| c. men calling out availability of massage parlor women | | | | | 66 | |
| d. photos at massage parlor entrances | | | | | 66 | |
| e. sounds/lights from adult theatres and topless bars | | | | | 53 | |
| f. topless/bottomless theatres | | | | | 64 | |
| Subtotal | 320 | 84 | 98 | 255 | 366 | 153 |
| **Part II** **Indirect Relationship** | | | | | | |
| g. prostitution noise at night | | | | 71 | | |
| h. cruising cars looking for pickups | | | | 69 | | |
| i. homosexual pickups | | | | 51 | | |
| j. transvestite solicitation | | | | 57 | | |
| Subtotal | 152 | 65 | 82 | 248 | 190 | 64 |
| TOTAL | 472 | 149 | 180 | 503 | 556 | 217 |

Remedy Rank
5. Pass legislation totally forbidding
4. Police should enforce existing laws
1. Pass legislation to keep off street
6. Organize local businessmen to put pressure
   on lawmakers about this
3. Citizen action: organize and demonstrate
2. Nothing

The preference for option 5 as a means of eliminating the nuisance aspects of adult entertainment, especially those items having an indirect relationship to adult activities, is consistent with earlier data result. The list of activities in Question 17 with the exception of (f), "topless and bottomless live theatres", duplicates the list given in Question 4 for offensiveness rating in Question 4: "solicitation by prostitutes and men calling out availability of massage parlor women," were designated for legislative solutions in Question 17.(See Table 6.3.)

The following group of graphs represents the choice of remedies as ranked by respondents for each of the ten items in Question 17. The contrast between Graph 1 and 6 demonstrates that regardless of the respondents' First Amendment attitude, there is a strong desire to interdict totally the adult entertainment industry. Very few respondents chose to do nothing and the number choosing to do nothing as a first choice remedy was insignificant. It is clear that the respondents have considerable faith in the legislative and enforcement mechanisms of the society to alleviate their distress in this matter.(See Graphs 1, 2, 3,.) This could be seen as an avoidance of direct action: when given the choice for some type of direct action, Graphs 4 and 5 show that the choice was low in rank.

Finally it can be seen that greater emphasis is placed on the role of enforcement in the area of abatement of nuisance, as shown in Graph 3. These nuisance areas comprise principally items 17 g) through 17 j). Interestingly, 17 e): "sounds/lights emanating from adult theatres

and topless bars" warranted a meaningful enforcement response,(3) while 17 f):  "topless and
bottomless live theatres" warranted a stronger
legislative response.

Graph No. 1 Remedy No. 5
Pass Legislation Totally Forbidding
R=No. of respondents

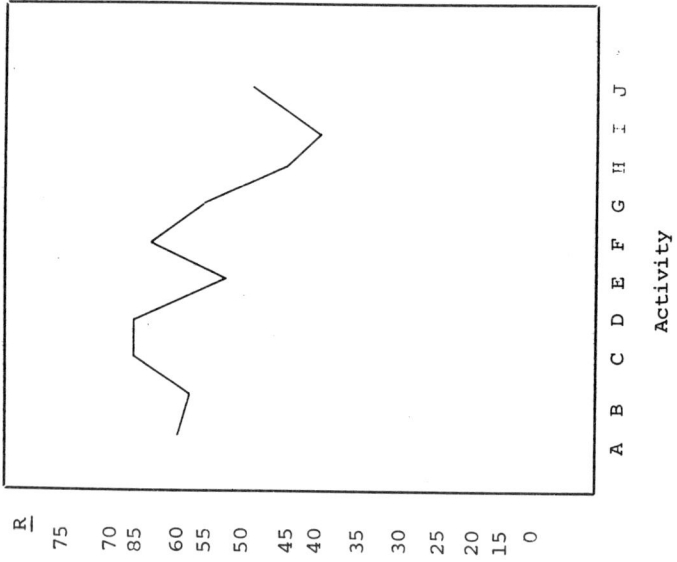

Graph No. 2 Remedy No. 1
Pass Legislation to Keep Off Street

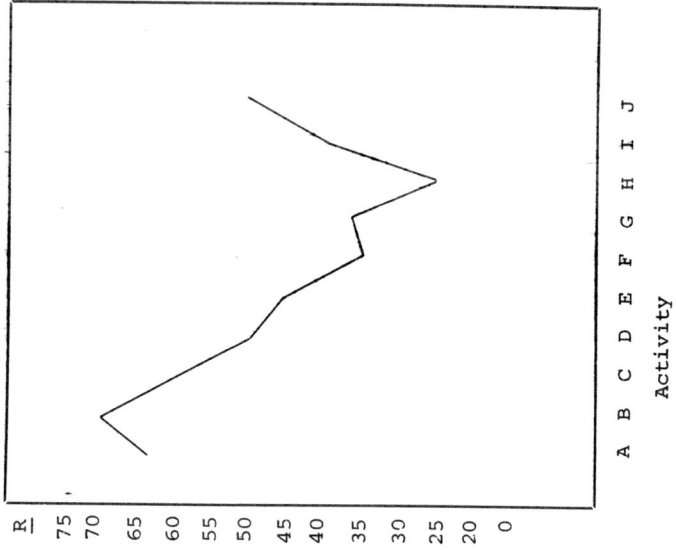

168

Graph No. 3    Remedy No. 4
Police Enforce Laws

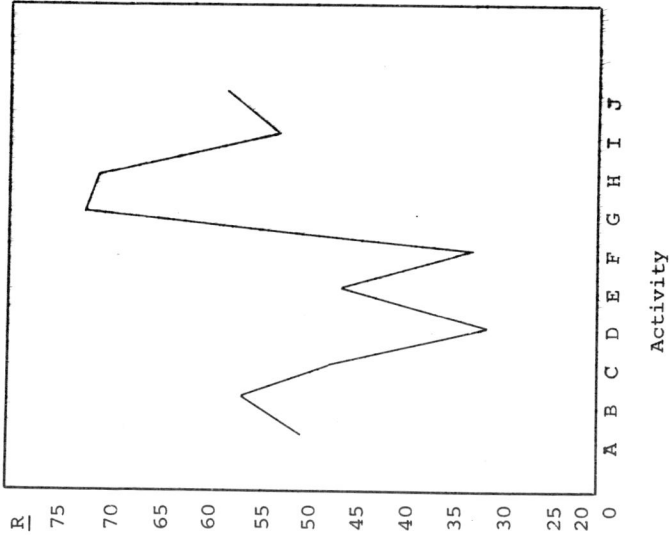

Graphy No. 4    Remedy No. 3
Citizen Action

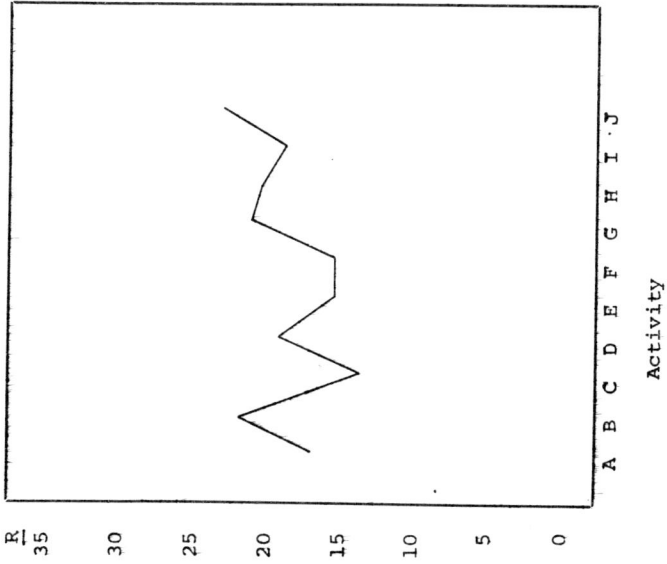

169

Graph No. 6    Remedy No. 2
Nothing

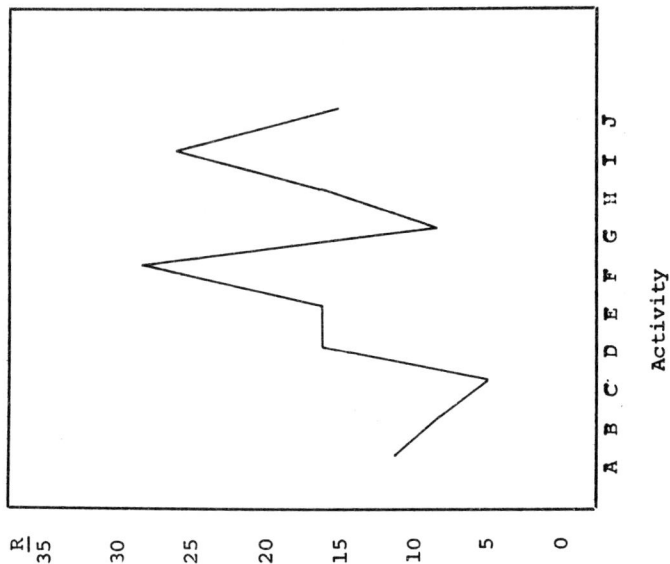

Graph No. 5    Remedy No. 6
Business Pressure

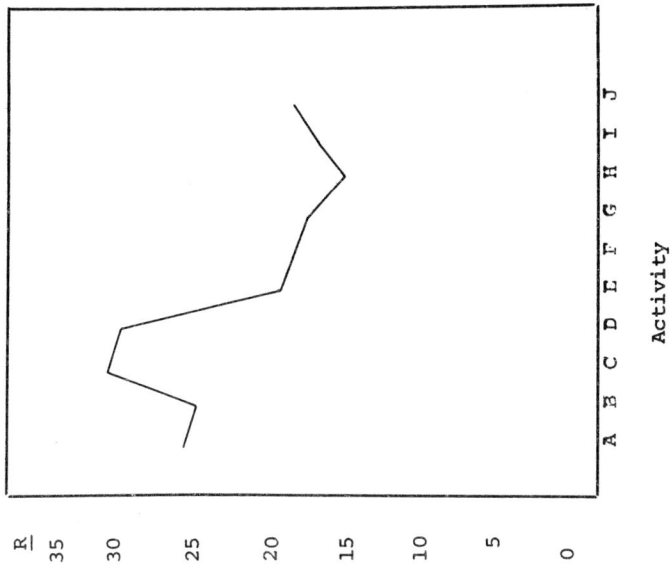

170

# FOOTNOTES

1.  New York City Planning Commission Calendar No.
    <u>23</u>. Jan. 26, 1977. N 760137 ZRY. "Amendments
    of the Zoning Resolution pursuant to Sec. 200
    of the New York City Charter relating to
    various sections concerning the definition of
    and regulation of adult uses." These Amendments
    are intended as an enforcement tool, and differ-
    entiate between two kinds of land uses:  x-rated
    (adult use) and others.  Essentially, it
    stipulates that no adult use shall be located
    within 500 feet of a residential district.
    Where two or more adult uses presently exist,
    no new uses may be established within an area
    1000 feet from the center of the zoning lot
    proposed, based on the new designation of
    adult use.  Proposed restrictions include:

    1.  no sign or window display shall specify
        sexual activity or area of body;

    2.  no adult use can have more than one acces-
        sory business sign except theatres which
        may have a marquee;

    3.  no advertising signs are permitted for
        adult use;

    4.  no sign for adult use may contain flashing
        lights of any sort, or extend beyond the
        street line, except for movie marquees;

    5.  all adult uses in districts not so desig-
        nated shall terminate within one year or
        effective date of the amendment.  As of
        the date of this writing, there has been
        sharp disagreement among the Borough
        Presidents as to the future implications of
        such an amendment:  Queens, the Bronx and

Staten Island would see an actual proli-
feration of pornography, and Brooklyn
would be completely protected from it, by
an "accident" in one of the Amendment's
provisions.

The mayoral election in the Fall of 1977, which
resulted in a new administration may be another
reason why this proposal has been lying dormant.

2. Charles Rembar. "Obscenity - Forget It".
   The Atlantic May, 1977. 37-41.

3. The New York Times 6/11/80 B1.

CHAPTER VII

DEMOGRAPHIC PROFILE AND RESPONSE

The demographic factors which delineate the survey population include age, education, income, marital status, occupation, race and sex. A number of these factors were examined to see whether they had any significance regarding the respondents' expression of offensiveness toward the adult entertainment industry.

The Pearson correlation technique was applied to the independent variables of age, education, and income.

## Age

It was expected that as age increases, offensiveness will increase, based upon the quotient of means in Question 3. Table 7.1 shows the correlation. The correlation is significant at the 0.02 level, indicating that as age increases, the offensiveness factor increases as well.

## Education

It was also expected that as education increases, offensiveness decreases. However, as Table 7.2 shows, the correlation coefficient is not significant at the 0.05 level. There is a negative correlation which means that respondents are still strongly offended as the level of education increases.

As can be seen from Table 7.3, there is no significant difference between Group A and Group B's First Amendment position, education level, and their attitudes toward the adult entertainment industry. Hence, the education level had no effect on respondents' liberality or severity toward constitutional protection for the operations of sex

TABLE 7.1.

Age/Offensiveness Quotient Correlation

| AGE | Coefficient 0.1649 | OFFENSIVENESS QUOTIENT |
|---|---|---|
| | N = 155 | Significance 0.020 |
| > | | |

TABLE 7.2.

Education/Offensiveness Quotient Correlation

| EDUCATION | Coefficient 0.0295 | OFFENSIVENESS QUOTIENT |
|---|---|---|
| | N = 155 | Significance 0.358 |
| > | | |

TABLE 7.3.

Percent of Respondents by Education Level
Cross Tabulated with First Amendment Position.

| First Amendment Position | Per Cent | Grade Sch. | Education Level Achieved High Sch. | College | Grad. Sch. | Row Total |
|---|---|---|---|---|---|---|
| Group A YES | 49.3 | 6.6 | 14.5 | 19.8 | .7.2 | 48.1 |
| Group B NO | 50.7 | 5.3 | 21.1 | 16.4 | 7.2 | 50.0 |
| Column Total | 100.0 | 11.9 | 35.6 | 36.2 | 14.4 | 98.1 |

businesses.  The mean level of education achievement for all respondents was 11.4 years.

## Income

Directly related to the above analysis was an effort on the part of researchers to determine if the income earned by respondents had any effect on respondents' attitudes toward First Amendment guarantees.  Results established that there was no significant difference by income on respondents' attitudes toward First Amendment protection for the adult entertainment industry.  This is consistent with the findings noted in Table 7.3. There is an equal chance that respondents would be equally divided on the basis of income on a First Amendment position.

The major significance of the findings based on the Pearson correlations and the education and income variables lies in the manifestation of a community solidarity on the adult entertainment issue which transcends the demographics of education and income.

## Race/Ethnicity

Given the ethnic diversity of Clinton, it was deemed important to ascertain if variations in ethnic responses to the survey would preclude the existence of a community consensus on the pornography issue.  The ethnic composition of Clinton as it emerged in the study is as follows: White, 80 per cent; Hispanic/Black, 19.3 per cent, and unidentified, 1.3 per cent.  Based on the division into White and Minority groupings, the respondents' answers were grouped into these categories:  overall sense of visibility of the

177

adult entertainment industry, based on Question 2; general offensiveness based on Question 3; and personal encounter with the industry, based on Question 4. The responses were submitted to a two-tailed probability T-test based on the means for each question.

For Questions 2, 3, and 4, Minority subjects were just as offended by the activity described in each question as were the non-minority subjects. This data confirms the presence of an overall community attitude on this issue which transcends racial or ethnic divisions. It should be added, however, that for Question 4, Hispanics registered a mean offensiveness of 8.3 while other Whites had a mean of 7.6. The difference approached significance at .058. As Hispanics represented about 12 per cent of the total sample, if the Hispanic segment were to be expanded, the probability is that this difference would become significant.

The Hispanic/Black subsample was divided into 60 per cent Hispanic and 33.3 per cent Blacks. Quotients based upon the means of their responses to Questions 2, 3, and 4 were submitted to the two-tailed probability T-test. The consistency of response was affirmed: there was no significant difference between these two groups.

The variable of sex did not affect the abstract consideration of First Amendment freedoms as they apply to those owning and purveying sex entertainments. Men and women were equally divided on the subject. In analyzing the mean offensiveness of women and men as a response to the list of sex businesses presented in Question 3, women's mean overall offensiveness was 6.1 as opposed to 4.9 for the men, at a significance level of 0.00. When presented with the street activities of pornographers in Question 4, women had a mean offensiveness of 8.0 and men 7.5, differences significant at the 0.04 level. Women are more offended than men both by the sex entertainments in themselves and by the advertising carried on in the streets. Yet while most respondents, male and female, would endorse women's activities to try to abate adult entertainment activity in Times Square and Clinton, the degree of public confidence accorded them in their own community is marginal, as shown in the comments accompanying Question 15.

It is one thing to tolerate "deviant" individual expression when it is widespread in space or widely interspersed in time. For those who reside next to Times Square, the question becomes more problematic. The sex industry there is highly concentrated and very visible. Question 7 shows that 60.3 per cent of respondents, whose overall profile is quite conservative toward adult entertainment, would continue to give a theatre family patronage even though it intersperses its mostly "G" rated film fare with x-rated films once in a while. They are willing to co-exist with sex businesses, to a reasonable degree, especially those which perform off the street and involve private, individual choice. However, a study of the questionnaire results and close observation of the temper of the Clinton population as a whole on this issue during the past two years as expressed in media interviews, demonstrations, and meetings, projects a feeling on their part that merely by living in Clinton, residents are being cheated somehow of the kind of life to which they voice allegiance: a traditional family neighborhood in

179

which many of them have lived from childhood, and which they fear will not be there much longer for their own children to enjoy. What gives special poignancy to the respondents' concern about children as expressed in the survey is the large number of runaway teenagers (and younger) who have surfaced as abused and exploited after having been lured into the Times Square prostitution business by pimps who promised them money and security. But this is a problem beyond the scope of this survey.(1)

No one can deny that the area in and around Times Square, with the exception of a few legitimate theatre blocks, is run down and deteriorating. Studies have shown that exposure to explicit sexual materials is not directly a cause of anti-social behavior. However, what needs to be done is a study on the effect of long-term exposure to pornographic materials - both for a "willing" and an "unwilling" audience. The majority of Clinton residents in the survey has shown in one way or another that over the years, as an "unwilling" audience to the sights and sounds related to adult entertainment, it has suffered harassment which could only be deleterious to mental health and detrimental to their neighborhood as expressed in replies and concerns in Question 19.

Table 7.4 reproduces Question 19 which requests the respondent to rank the seriousness of problems related to and created by the adult entertainment industry. Interviewers were instructed to write replies in rank order 1 - 3 on blanks provided at left. In presenting responses, only those which fell into first, second, or third ranking order are presented in Table 7.5.

It becomes immediately clear that problem statements four and seven are uppermost in the minds of the respondents. Number 4, neighborhood deterioration, is regarded as the most serious effect upon

TABLE 7.4.

List of Problems Related to the
Adult Entertainment Industry.

RANK                                    ISSUE

0    Prostitution on 8th and 10th Avenues
1    Undue Attention
2    Spread of sex businesses to the '50's
3    Street harassment
4    Neighborhood deterioration
5    Politicians' self-interest
6    Sexual attitudes
7    Effect on children
8    Unconstitutional solutions
9    Support of organized crime

181

the Clinton community of the pornographic trade.
This is tantamount to saying that adult entertainment directly contributes to neighborhood deterioration.  There is consistency with responses to
Questions 2, 3, 4, 6, and 11, and it probably
accounts in some degree for the high level of negative public attitudes toward this industry.

Second choice was statement No. 7:  effect on
children.  This is consistent with the fact that
28 respondents have 67 children under age 17 among
them.  Thus, there is a high percentage of children
in the survey population, or 43 per cent.  This
indicates that more families with children responded
to the survey than is true for the population
universe sampled.(2)  It also accounts for the
concern for the effect of the adult entertainment
industry on children in the area, which is still
thought of by respondents as a "family" neighborhood.  Another factor which might have contributed
to this result was the extensive media campaigns
which were being mounted during the survey, concerning the use of very young children in pornographic productions.  Several demonstrations on
the part of Phoenix House residents and staff in
front of 42nd Street bookstores carrying "kiddie
porn" publications such as "Lollitots" received
wide public attention.  The importance given to
the effect on children might also relate to
popular belief that there is a negative impact
to be expected when pornography is made accessible
to impressionable youth.

The presence of this industry is also viewed
as militating against community stability; thus,
respondents feel that Clinton is not a desirable
place to raise children.

TABLE 7.5.

Ranking of Three Most Serious Problems
Related to the Adult Entertainment Industry
in Times Square Area.

RANKED ORDER NUMBER

|  | 1 | 2 | 3 |
|---|---|---|---|
| First Choice Statement No. | 4 | 7 | 3 |
| Per Cent | 31.5 | 26.2 | 19.9 |
| Second Choice Statement No. | 7 | 4 | 7 |
| Per Cent | 25.9 | 23.8 | 19.1 |
| Third Choice Statement No. | 0 | 0 | 4 |
| Per Cent | 20.3 | 14.6 | 17.6 |

The third most serious problem was street harassment. Clearly this harassment aspect might be considered a summary response to all the preceding items. Harassment epitomizes the effect of living with pornographic street activities, especially prostitution, leafletting, or photographs advertising sexually-oriented entertainments. These aspects of the sex industry merited the higher offensiveness ratings by survey participants.

## Summary

Demographic Profile and Response. A number of demographic factors of the survey population were examined to see whether they had any significance regarding the respondents' expression of offensiveness toward the adult entertainment industry. The Pearson correlation technique was applied to the independent variables of age, education, and income. It was expected that as age increases, offensiveness will increase, based upon the quotient of means from the question dealing with offensiveness. Correlation was significant at the .02 level, indicating that as age increases, the offensiveness factor increases as well. It was also expected that as education increases, offensiveness would decrease. However, the Pearson result was a negative correlation, which means that respondents are still strongly offended as the level of education increases. For education level achieved, cross tabulation was applied to the two groups with opposing First Amendment positions. Results showed that education level had no effect on respondents' liberality or severity toward constitutional protection for the operators of sex businesses. It was determined that there was also no significant difference by income on respondents' attitudes toward First Amendment protections for the adult entertainment industry; the total group does not divide on the

First Amendment position, based on income level.

The major significance of the findings based
on the Pearson correlations and the education
and income variables lies in the manifestation of
a community solidarity on the adult entertainment
issue which transcends these demographics.  It
was expected that as these two variables increased
offensiveness would decrease.

Given the ethnic diversity of Clinton, it was
deemed important to ascertain if variations in
ethnic responses to the survey would preclude
the existence of a community consensus on the
pornography issue.  The ethnic composition of
Clinton as it emerged in the study is as follows:
White, 80 percent; Hispanic/Black, 19.3 percent,
and unidentified, 1.3 percent.  Based on the
division into White and Minority groupings, the
respondents' replies were grouped into these
categories: overall sense of visibility of the
adult entertainment industry; general offensiveness; and personal encounter with adult activities
based on the relevant questions for each category.
The replies were submitted to a two-tailed probability t-test based on the means for such questions.

Statistical analysis showed that minority
subjects were just as offended by the activity
described in each category as were non-minority
subjects.  This data confirms the presence of an
overall community sentiment on this issue.  It
should be added, however, that for the question
dealing with means of offensiveness, Hispanics
registered a mean offensiveness of 8.3, while
other Whites had a mean of 7.7.  The difference
approached significance at .058.  Since Hispanics
represented about 12 percent of the total sample,
if the Hispanic segment were to be expanded, the
probability is that this difference would become

185

significant. The Hispanic/Black subsample was
divided into 60 percent Hispanics and 33.3
percent Black. Quotients based on the personal
experience of the adult industry were submitted
to the two-tailed t-test. The consistency of the
response was affirmed: there was no significant
difference between these two groups.

The variable of sex did not affect the abstract
consideration of First Amendment freedoms as they
apply to those owning and purveying sex entertainments. Men and women were equally divided on the
subject. However, it anticipated that women would
be more offended by adult activities. In analyzing
mean offensiveness of women and men as a response
to a list of sex businesses presented in one
question, women's mean offensiveness was 6.1, as
opposed to 4.9 for the men; at a significance level
of 0.00. When presented with the street activities
of pornographers, women had a mean offensiveness of
8.0 and men 7.5; differences significant at the
0.04 level. Women are more offended than men both
by the sex entertainments in themselves and
by the advertising carried on in the streets.

It is one thing to tolerate "deviant" individual expression when it is widespread in space or
widely interspersed in time. The Supreme Court
decision regarding Erznoznik v. Jacksonville did
not recognize film nudity as a potential nuisance
because it was shown in one outdoor movie house in
the city, and was easily avoidable. For those residing next to Times Square, the question becomes
more problematic. The sex industry there is highly
concentrated and very visible. Yet when asked,
60.3 percent of the respondents, whose overall
profile is quite conservative toward the question
of adult entertainment, would continue to give a
theatre family patronage even though it occasionally

186

intersperses its mostly "G"-rated film fare with x-rated films.

They seem willing to co-exist with sex businesses to a reasonable degree, expecially those shows which perform off the street, and involve private individual choice. However, a study of the questionnaire results and close observation of the temper of the Clinton population as a whole on this issue during the past two years, as expressed in media interviews, demonstrations and meetings projects a feeling that merely by living here, the residents are being cheated somehow of the kind of life to which they voice allegiance: a traditional family neighborhood, in which many of them have lived from childhood, and which they fear will not be there much longer for their own children to enjoy.

No one can deny that the atmosphere in and around Times Square, with the exception of a few legitimate theatre blocks, is depressing and even menacing. Studies have shown that exposure to explicit sexual materials is not directly a cause of anti-social behavior. .

A study needs to be carried out on the effect of long-term exposure to pornographic materials - both for a "willing" and an "unwilling" audience. The majority of Clinton residents in the survey has shown in one way or another that it believes itself an "unwilling" audience to the sights and sounds related to adult entertainment street activity, and it has suffered harassment which could only be deleterious to mental health and detrimental to their neighborhood.

The last question requests that respondents rank in 1,2,3 order of seriousness problems related to and created by the adult entertainment

industry. Uppermost in the minds of residents was
neighborhood deterioration, ranked the number 1
related problem. This is equal to saying that
adult entertainment directly contributes to
neighborhood deterioration. There is consistency
here with responses to Questions 2,3,4,6, and 11,
and it probably accounts in some degree for high
level of negative public opinion towards this
industry. Second-ranked problem was the effect
on children of sex businesses. This is consistent
with the fact that 28 respondents have 67 children
under age 17 among them. There is a high percentage of children in the survey population, (43 per
cent). This indicates that more families with
children responded to the survey than is true for
the population universe.(3) It also accounts for
the concern and for the effect of the adult entertainment industry on children in the area, which is
still thought of by respondents as a "family"
neighborhood. Another factor which might have
contributed to this result was the extensive media
campaigns being mounted during the survey concerning the use of very young children in pornographic productions. The importance given to the
effect on children might also relate to popular
belief that there is a negative impact to be
expected when pornography is made accessible to
impressionable youth. The presence of this industry is also viewed as militating against community
stability; thus, respondents feel that Clinton is
not a desirable place to raise children.

The third-ranked serious problem was street
harassment. Clearly, this harassment aspect might
be considered a summary response to all the preceding items having to do with pornographic street
activities, especially prostitution, leafletting,
or photographs advertising sexually-oriented
entertainments. These aspects of the sex industry
merited the higher offensiveness ratings by survey
participants.

## FOOTNOTES

1. Dorothy Bracey, <u>Baby Pros</u>. New York: John Jay Press, 1979.

2. According to 1970 U.S. Census figures for Tracts 115, 121, 127, and 133 in Clinton, there were 3,545 children under 17 years of age living in the area at that time, or 17% of the population of these four tracts.

3. See footnote 2, above.

CHAPTER VIII

CONCLUSIONS AND RECOMMENDATIONS

This study attempted to give the sample of voters opportunity to do two things: express their feelings about the presence of commercial sex activities in their midst, and to indicate how these activities might be better regulated than at present. Because the respondents have indicated that the activities connected with Times Square sex businesses as they presently exist are a threat to their longstanding chosen lifestyle, legislation and enforcement of nuisance abatement in a permanent, ongoing way are essential.

The responses as a whole give the impression that participants in the survey see themselves as being influential in bringing stability and character to their Clinton neighborhood. One of the factors contributing to the conservative profile of the respondents regarding adult entertainment activities is their mean length of residence in Clinton - 21.1 years. Long-term commitment to a place of residence in this case seems to account for a more severe attitude toward perceived deviation from a family lifestyle.

Since these respondents are probably fairly representative of the voting population as a whole for the Clinton area sampled, then abatement of the aggressive manner in which street activities of adult entertainments are carried on will reassure them that their lifestyle has a future in Clinton. It is precisely this result which will prove the effectiveness of this study; but which can only be brought about by the speedy response of legislative and law enforcement agencies, both municipal and state.

To determine the consensus on nuisance, the components of the nuisance statute, Penal Law Sec. 1530 were examined. (See infra, "Terms" in Chapter 2.) The principal components of the nuisance definition include: 1) annoyance 2) offensiveness 3) interference and 4) insecurity in person and property. Clearly, the residents of Clinton are experiencing all four aspects of a nuisance. Question 6 delineates annoyance with public advertising of adult entertainment events, with a demand for remedy. The strong objection to the street activities in question either as definitely or probably not allowable expresses the level of community annoyance.

Question 8 shows the respondents sensitivity to the issues of health and safety, as an aspect of part one of the nuisance definition. The respondents showed a degree of sophistication, as shown in Table 4.4 and 4.6 in that they could distinguish between false advertising and fire hazards, as opposed to mere contrivances of the law, as grounds for closing down sex businesses.

Question 4 and 6 illustrate the community's response to the obstruction and interference aspects of the sex businesses themselves, and their manner of advertising. The responses to 4 a), b), c), g) and 6 f), g), h), are an indication of the offensiveness expressed by the community regarding some of these activities.

The offensiveness aspect of nuisance was borne in mind when an "offensiveness scale" was designed in Question 3 for a rating of nine different adult entertainment businesses, and in Question 4, which asked for a rating of nine related activities as experienced in the streets

of the area. Thus offensiveness ratings were
obtained for both the businesses as perceived in
themselves, and for experience of the street
activities of the sex industry in the Clinton-
Times Square neighborhood.

In Question 3, the lowest mean offensiveness
was for the bookstore item (5.9), while the
highest was for the item on prostitute solicitation (7.8). The overall generalized offensiveness
mean for Question 3 is 6.686, indicating a middling
degree of offensiveness when considering sex
businesses per se. Question 4 dealt with personal
experience of the street activities of the adult
entertainment industry. The overall experience
mean is 7.541, which demonstrates that the respondents are clearly bothered or annoyed, conform-
able to part one of the nuisance definition,
by the adult entertainment industry's related
activities. It becomes clear that the high visibility and "interference" aspects of these
activities are most troublesome to residents.

Responses to Question 4 d), e), f), and 6 a),
b), c), d) illustrate the sense of insecurity which
aggressive styles of operating sex businesses
can bring to residents of the area. This element
of threat to the respondents is finally affirmed in
Question 19, where the sample perceived the
deterioration of the neighborhood (4) and effect
on children (7), along with prostitution activity
(0) as the most critical issues related to the
presence of the adult entertainment industry.

In establishing that the adult entertainment
activities selected for this study meet all the
criteria of nuisance, is also becomes important
to assess the visible aspect of the activity on
the Clinton community prior to measurement of

193

offensiveness. Question 2 inquired about visibility (See Table 3.12). It was determined that respondents found the sex businesses highly visible: 18 per cent or less of respondents on all items indicated fewer "adult" businesses existed in the area during the previous year. To some this may seem self-evident; to others, the visibility of the adult entertainment industry is rooted in the politics of election year, notoriety, campaigns against using advertising photos of women being abused, kiddie porn, and intensive media coverage of these events.

While the visibility of the adult entertainment industry is reasonably self-evident to residents, researchers undertook to document the actual extent of its presence during the year 1977. The businesses were grouped and enumerated by the researchers in a walking survey and compared with the figures from the Midtown Planning Office data (See Table 3.13). Then the operational data was compared to the respondents surveyed as a perception of intensity; i.e., that the industry was more or less visible.

In Questions 4 and 6, respondents were asked to state how they felt about selected samples of visible activity or businesses in terms of the meaning and purpose of the enterprises; i.e., while recognizing that advertising is a necessary part of any business, how do the respondents assess the adult entertainment industry's street activities in the Clinton community? The overall responses were negative, and those to Question 6 expressed desire for a high degree of regulation (See Table 3.14) of the visible aspects of sex businesses.

Question 11 enabled the respondents to candidly assess the visible impact of three selected businesses in the area which typify "adult" enterprises. While the respondents expressed a degree of tolerance for the sex industry insofar as it may generate some jobs (11b) and provide a service (11h), the general attitude on the visibility for these businesses is negative. Hence while such services may serve some, they should not be "thrust" upon the public - the community - in a vulgar and tawdry manner. To this extent, the respondents want zoning restrictions (Question 16) on the number of enterprises and their proximity to a residential area.

These businesses were seen as engaging in false advertising, non-compliance with the fire code, and staffed with unlicensed personnel (Question 8). All these matters fall within the regulatory powers of the City.

Analysis of the results of Question 17 shows that the survey population expects legislative and enforcement action before community action. This suggests that those surveyed do not perceive clearly the dynamic relationship between community action and appropriate governmental response. Related to the weak profile respondents have drawn of themselves as a political force are the responses given to Question 18, where nine categories of community leadership were presented with individual names for each category for recognition and evaluation by each respondent. Only one name was recognized by more that 50 percent of the respondents, that of Rev. Robert Rappelyea of Holy Cross Catholic Church, who had led neighborhood demonstrations within the community on pornography issues.

It is therefore plausible to affirm the view that the citizens of Clinton will exert pressure for demonstrable change. Change is desired. Question 17 shows that the community points to strict legislation to totally forbid or to keep certain "adult" activities off the street, followed by police enforcement of existing laws. Only after these preferred alternatives would community action ensue. The community does not see itself as the prime mover in this form of social change; rather, it places its confidence in established legislative and enforcement processes.

The findings warrant the researchers' conclusions that there are demonstrable nuisance and harrassment aspects to the Clinton view of the adult entertainment industry, and that change is demanded by the community. The primary place for legal remedy to be implemented is in the Assembly in Albany and City Hall in New York. Finally, police enforcement of the necessary nuisance laws should reduce the need for citizen campaigns and business pressure.

The respondents' answers indicate clearly they will exert pressure on the legislature, the City Council and the police to effect change. Of course, this has been done before by small groups of concerned residents, representing an unknown quantity of people in the Clinton area. It can be said that all the voters residing in Clinton are articulating a desire for long range involvement in effecting this change.

Findings of equally high significance are present in the respondents perceptions of the legality of the adult entertainment businesses in the abstract and in situ. The respondents dislike for sex businesses and attendant activities does not establish alone adequate grounds for their demise. In Chapter IV an effort was made to relate the community's negative attitude for the street aspects of adult entertainment with perceived legality of the industry. What emerged is a generally balanced judgment of the community on a question which in most respondents' minds is emotionally charged. Given this emotional atmosphere, it must be concluded that because respondents accept that there is some need for this business, that it does have a place, that it affords some employment locally, their responses have a greater credibility. Respondents could also thoughtfully distinguish between acceptable and unacceptable grounds for closure, discriminately rank activities and apply rational solutions. The participants divided almost evenly: 50.7 vs. 49.3 percent on First Amendment attitudes toward the adult entertainment industry. Hence, it is established that in the abstract, there is no clearly uniform judgment against the industry. What the study shows is that when the respondents were asked to judge each specific activity as part of or attendant upon the adult entertainment industry, there was a significant shift in position. It could be said that those respondents who experienced the shift are affirming their right to carry on the avowed lifestyle without annoyance or insecurity thrust upon them by purveyors of commercial sex. These respondents are voicing the most important question raised by this project: if, in the process of upholding First Amendment rights for one interest group, another group perceives that its interests are disparaged and threatened, can legal remedies be brought to bear on the situation to bring it into better balance for both groups concerned?

The Clinton-Times Square Survey's approach has been to deal principally with the phenomenon of the "unwilling audience" in adult entertainment. It has attempted to determine just how "unwilling" an audience the Clinton community is regarding its experience with the street aspects of the sex industry. While not a major recommendation, it is noteworthy that the Commission on Obscenity and Pornography in 1970 advocated the passage of "public display" laws in each state, designed to protect unwilling viewers from offensive depiction of sexual activity, when these displays can be seen from a public street or sidewalk or from the property of others. This covers primarily display windows, displays outside of theatres, billboards, and outdoor theatre screens when visible from the highway or other property. Nudity is not forbidden except when genitals are emphasized.

## Recommendations

1. This report has tried to show that definitions of obscenity are thus far unclear, and that nuisance statutes providing for injunctive relief against sex businesses are based on determinations of obscenity, or are struck down as repressive of First Amendment freedoms. Legislators need to consider the balance of conflicting rights - First Amendment, and those of preserving the character of a community as articulated by a sampling of its resident voters, as a significant basis for injunctive action vs. sex businesses. In drafting remedial legislation for the Times Square area, lawmakers have in this study the

collective sentiment of offensiveness to high visibility of adult entertainments on the part of participants.

2. Results of the survey have demonstrated that the resident voting population is largely ignorant of their local political and community leadership. They neither know them by name, nor what is their position on important public issues. Regardless of what the problem is to be addressed within Clinton, the leadership suffers from a serious image gap. Leaders of Community Board 4, the Clinton Planning Coucil, and the local political parties might address themselves to remedying this lack of knowledge in their constituents. This constituency is not apathetic when its life-style is threatened. The Clinton community put forth energetic efforts which blocked the conversion of the Manhattan Plaza Project to low-income housing.

3. The local leadership will find the most effective means of raising community consciousness on the issues of adult entertainment by addressing itself to the three major threats which respondents expressly related to the sex industry: deterioration of the neighborhood, the effect of this industry on the lives of their children, and the street harassment experienced in going about the Clinton-Times Square area.

4. The disparity encountered in methods of presenting and storing data on the part of the City Board of Health and Police Headquarters, and Midtown agencies with special assignments of monitoring the adult entertainment industry was a significant obstacle to compiling accurate statistics concerning crime rate, venereal disease rate, and a count of pornographic establishments of

Times Square. Uniform jurisdictions and reporting of data would contribute greatly to a more accurate representation of complex social processes as they occur over a period of time. This would enable those who study these social problems to formulate more realistic theories on causation.

## Directions for Further Research

1. This study might be repeated with a random representative sample of the entire Clinton population, to see whether results are significantly different regarding attitudes on offensiveness and visibility of the industry, suggested remedies for adult street advertising, and an appraisal of problems related to pornographic businesses.

2. Since the adult entertainment industry is largely an urban problem because of its scope, intensity and variety of expression, an analysis of the environmental aspect of this industry offers fruitful avenue for socio-legal investigation of the question: "Does long-term continuous high visibility of pornographic materials in public advertising for x-rated businesses have an adverse effect on the mental health of the 'unwilling audience' living in its midst?"

3. Responses to Questions 9 and 10 suggest that various Times Square entertainments are ranked according to the social status of those involved in producing them. Further study on this could be done, based on Gusfield's theory linking anti-pornography crusades with status politics.

4. From the feminist point of view, Questions 13, 14, and 15 tried to address the question of the female image in the rock record industry and in the

mind of the Clinton Sample; however, the questions as phrased do not lend themselves to theoretical elaboration. We do know that women had both a higher generalized mean score and experience offensiveness mean score than did men in Questions 3 and 4. Future study might attempt to discover why this is so.

# BIBLIOGRAPHY

Black's Law Dictionary. West Publishing Co.,
    St. Paul, Minn. (1968): 1215.

Bracey, Dorothy. "Baby-Pros." John Jay Press,
    N.Y. (1979).

Censorship News. No. 4, September 1977: 5-6

Chambliss, W.J. & Siedman, R.B. Law, Order and
    Power. Addison Wesley Co., Mass. (1971).

Chappelle, Pamela. "Can an adult theatre or
    bookstore be abated as a public nuisance in
    California?" University of San Francisco
    Law Review, Vol. 10: 115-132, Summer 1975.

Chelsea-Clinton News. Sept. 22, 1977:2
    _____. February 9, 1978: 1 & 3.

Chicago Tribune. June 27, 1976. Editorial page.

City of New York Administrative Code. Vol. 3:301.
    Williams Press, Albany N.Y. (1969)

City Planning Commission Calendar No. 23. Jan.28,
    1977. N760137ZRY. "Amendments of Zoning
    Resolution Pursuant to Sec. 200 of N.Y.C.
    Charter re Definition and Regulation of
    Adult Uses.

Cohen, D. "Pornography and Crime: A New Look."
    Atlas World Press Review. Dec. 1976: 26-27.

Colson, C.E. "The Evaluation of Pornography:
    Effects of Attitude and Perceived Physiolo-
    gical Reaction". Archives of Sexual Behavior,
    Vol. 34: 307-323. July 1974.

Council of the City of New York. Local Law No. 55f 1977. Int. No. 1880. June 21, 1977

De Grazia, ed. Censorship Landmarks. R.R. Bowker Co., N.Y. (1969): 94-101.

Erznoznik v. City of Jacksonville. U.S. Supreme Court Reports. Lawyers' Ed. 2nd Series, Vol. 45:2268 et seq.

Gerber, A.B. Sex, Pornography & Justice. New York (1965).

Goldstein, M. & Kant, H.S. Pornography & Sexual Deviance. Univ. of Cal. Press (1973).

Gusfield, J.R. Symbolic Crusade: Status Politics and the American Temperance Movement. Univ. of Illinois Press, Urbana (1963).

Hamling v. U.S. U.S. Supreme Court Reports. Vol. 590. Lawyers Cooperative Publ. Co. Rochester N.Y. (1975).

Hunter, I.A. "Obscenity, Pornography & Law Reform." Dalhousie Law Journal, Vol. 2:482-504. May 1975

Jacobson, Nancy G. "Restricting Public Display of Offensive Materials: Use and Effectiveness of Public and Private Nuisance Actions." Univ. of San Francisco Law Review, Vol. 10:232-251. Fall 1975

Kingsley Pictures Corp. v. Regents. U.S. Supreme Court Reports, Vol. 360:684-689. (1959)

Kirkpatrick, R.G. "Collective Consciousness and Mass Hysteria: Collective Behavior and Anti-Pornography Crusades in Durkheimian Perspective". Human Relations, Vol. 28:63-84. Feb. 1975.

Lawrence, D.H. "Pornography & Obscenity". The Outcast Chapbooks, No. 13. Alicat Bookshop, Yonkers, N.Y. (1948)

Lockhart, Wm.B. "Escape from the Chill of Uncertainty: Explicit Sex and the First Amendment". Georgia Law Review, Vol 9, No. 3:533-79. Spring 1975.

_____. "Findings and Recommendations of the Commission on Obscenity and Pornography: A Case Study of the Role of Social Science in Formulating Public Policy". Oklahoma Law Review, Vol. 24:209-223. 1971

Meyer, Timothy P. "The Effects of Sexually Arousing and Violent Films on Aggressive Behavior". Journal of Sex Research, Vol. 8, No. 4:324-331. Nov. 1972.

Miller v. California. U.S. Supreme Court Reports, Vol. 413:15. (1973)

New York Jurisprudence. Vol. 42:443-572. Lawyers Cooperative Publishing Co., Rochester, N.Y. (1965)

New York Law Journal. "City of N.Y. v. 1173 Sixth Bldg. Co. Inc." Nov. 3, 1977:7.

_____. "Law v. Social Science." Nov. 15, 1977:4.

_____. "People v. Peter Ventrice." July 21, 1978:8.

New York Times. Sept. 14, 1976:39.

_____. Nov. 1, 1976:14.

_____. Nov. 15, 1976:37.

_____. Dec. 27, 1976. "Essay" Op. Ed. page.

_____. Feb. 7, 1977. Op. Ed. page.

_____. Mar. 6, 1977. Magazine Sec.:18 et
    seq.

_____. Mar. 9, 1977:27.

_____. Apr. 6, 1977:23.

_____. Apr. 11, 1977. op. Ed. page.

_____. Apr. 13, 1977. Sec. B:1,4.

_____. Apr. 14, 1977:24.

_____. Apr. 20, 1977. op. Ed. page.

_____. Apr. 22, 1977. Sec. A:28.

_____. May 17, 1977. Editorial page.

_____. May 19, 1977.   "   "   "

_____. June 13, 1977: 1 and 19.

_____. June 14, 1977:48.

_____. June 21, 1977. Editorial page.

_____. July 1, 1977.   "   "   "

_____. July 27, 1977: 1 and A13.

_____. Oct. 10, 1977:26.

_____. June 11, 1980. B1.

O'Connor, P.J. "The Nuisance Abatement Law as a
     Solution to N.Y.C.'s Problem of Illegal Sex
     Related Businesses in the Midtown Area."
     Fordham Law Review, Vol. XLVI, No. 1. (Oct.
     1977).

Oxford English Dictionary. Vol. VII. Oxford (1961).

Rembar, Charles. Perspectives. Arbor House,
     N.Y. (1975).

_____. "Obscenity - Forget It". The
     Atlantic. May, 1977:37-41.

Rendelman, Douglas. "Civilizing Pornography:
     The Case for An Exclusive Obscenity Nuisance
     Statute." University of Chicago Law Review,
     Vol. 44, No. 3:509-560. Spring 1977.

Rist, Ray C. The Pornography Controversy. Trans-
     actions Books, New Brunswick, N.J. (1975).

Schopler, E.H. "Supreme Court's Development Since
     Roth v. U.S. of Standards and Principles
     Determining the Concept of Obscenity in the
     Context of Right of Free Speech and Press."
     U.S. Supreme Court Reports, Lawyers' Ed. 2nd
     Series, Vol. 41:1257-1293.

Sharp, Donald B., ed. Commentaries on Obscenity.
     Scarecrow Press. N.J. (1970).

Smelser, N.J. Theory of Collective Behavior. N.Y.
     Free Press (1962).

Smith v. U.S. U.S. Law Week, Vol. 45:4495-4503
     May 23, 1977.

The Report on Obscenity and Pornography. U.S.
     Commission on Obscenity and Pornography
     U.S. Gov't. Printing Office Document (1970)

Wallace, D.H. "A Survey on Obscenity and Contem-
     porary Community Standards". Journal of
     Social Issues: Vol 29, No. 3:53-67. (1973).

Young v. The American Mini-Theatre Inc. Official
     Reports of the Supreme Court, Vol. 427, Pt.
     1:50-96.

Zett, Jas. N.Y. Criminal Practice, Vol. 10. M.
     Bender, N.Y. 1976.

Zurcher, L.A. & Kirkpatrick, R.G. Citizens for
     Decency: Anti-Pornography Crusades as Status
     Defense. Univ. of Texas Press, Austin. (1976)

Edward J. Shaughnessy, is an Associate Professor of Sociology at the John Jay College of Criminal Justice and the University Graduate Center with a specialization in law. He has directed The Institute for Legal and Criminal Justice Education at the John Jay College, under federal subsidy. He had edited the New York State Bar Association's Law Studies and is the author of several articles on terrorism. Shaughnessy is currently preparing a manuscript on pre-trial problems in criminal court and another on terrorism. He has served as Training Coordinator for the Division of Criminal Justice Services of New York State. He has been awarded a Fulbright to Norway to study dispute resolution in criminal cases under the auspices of The Institute for Criminology and Criminal Law University of Oslo.

Diana Trebbi, survey director, is a doctoral
student in sociology at the City University of
New York, Graduate Center. Ms. Trebbi received
a grant to study the history of linguistic patterns
in France. She has worked with women's groups
since 1956. In 1974 Ms. Trebbi helped to form
the N.Y. Women's Ordination Conference, a group
whose goal is to further the status of women in
the American Catholic Church. Recently, she
has worked with Rockefeller Foundation programs
devoted to studying problems of world food supply
and population. She has served as editor of the
Hispanic page and board member of The Clinton
Community Press. Currently, Ms. Trebbi is
associated with Interfaith Women, a group formed to
launch a new publication devoted to furthering
the position of women in the major Western religions.

# AFTERWORD

In the two years since the Clinton-Times Square study was published, pornographic businesses in the midtown area have experienced a continuing decline in number. The greatest decrease has been in massage parlors. At the end of 1977, there were 27 in the area; at last count in September, 1979 there were 14 according to The New York Times of November 18, 1979. The site of the massage parlor, 1173 Avenue of the Americas, whose history is reviewed in this study, has been closed. Seymour Durst, owner of the property housing the massage parlor, remarked that the legal work cost almost as much as the entire property. In the end, the shop "just moved out", he said, a reflection of the changed market for pornography. Related to the drop in massage parlors is the almost total disappearance of men passing out the leaflets advertising the services of women. With the decrease in massage parlors has come a new category of sex entertainment: the "facility" for "swingers". Since the end of 1977, two sex facilities have opened in midtown, according to the Midtown Law Enforcement Project.

As a result of the net decrease in concentration of the pornographic industry in Times Square, the street environment has improved. The lower visibility of the industry may be due perhaps to assiduous law enforcement and the vagaries of supply and demand. The ready availability of home "porn" on videotape may have some momentary significance in this regard. Hollywood is testing the perimeters of the "R" or Restricted category of film with such works as "The Blues Brothers" and "Dressed to Kill". From 39th Street to 45th Street, and from the Avenue of the Americas to Eighth Avenue, donut shops, photo labs, jewelry stores, messenger services and delicatessens have replaced former pornographic trade sites.

Public awareness of the problems raised
by a concentration of sex-related businesses
is now much higher than when our study began.
There are even tours to the sites of the
adult entertainment industry as a consciousness
raising activity. Street environment problems
still persist in the form of peddlers, gambling
activities, crime, drug sales and pandering in
the face of the efforts made to effect lasting
improvement in the Times Square area. The
climate of change seems to forecast improvement
in the quality of life.

## Appendix I

Clinton (---) is legally defined as comprising the area bounded by 8th to 12th Avenues, and 34th to 59th Streets inclusive. The portion of Clinton included in the survey is only that area which directly overlaps Times Square in U.S. 1970 census tracts 0115, 0121, 0127, and 0133. It is wholly or partly encompassed by Election Districts Nos. 6, 7, 11, 12, 13, 14, 15, 16, 17.

Times Square (——) is designated as the U.S. census tracts Nos. 0113, 0115, 0119, 0121, 0125, 0127, 0131, 0133. This area is a political, geographic division of New York City, encompassing parts of the 20th Congressional District, the 27th State Senatorial District, the 67th State Assembly District, and the 3rd City Council District. It is wholly or partly encompassed by Election Districts Nos. 6, 7, 8, 9, 10, 11, 12, 13, 14, 15, , 16, 17, 18, 80.

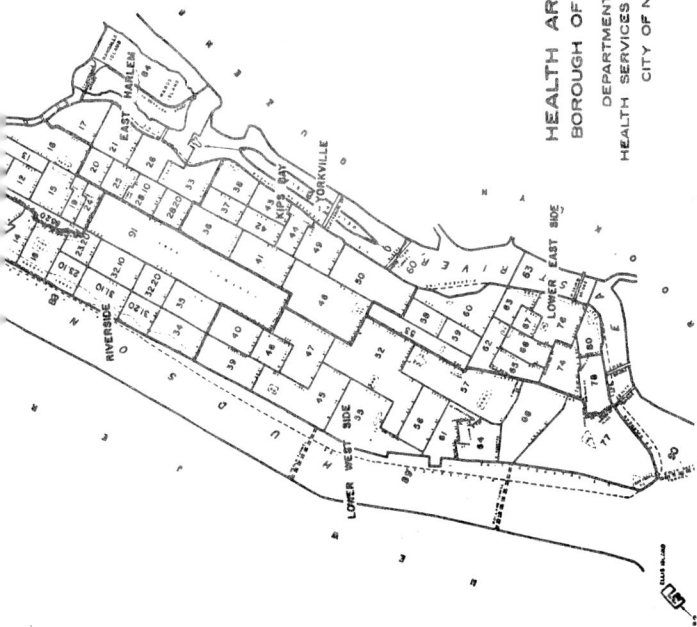

HEALTH AREAS — 1972
BOROUGH OF MANHATTAN
DEPARTMENT OF HEALTH
HEALTH SERVICES ADMINISTRATION
CITY OF NEW YORK

Appendix III

Clinton-Times Square Survey
April 15 - June 30, 1977.

Block Numbering and Block Concentration
of Survey Population

214

Respondent I. D. No. _____

| 26, 27, 28/ |
| --- |

— CLINTON TIMES SQUARE PROJECT —

SURVEY OF COMMUNITY PERCEPTION
OF IMPACT OF TIMES SQUARE
ADULT ENTERTAINMENT INDUSTRY

Time interview began: _____A. M. _____P. M.

Date: _____

Interviewer's Name: _____

No. _____

INTRODUCTION. How do you do. I'm _____ and I'm working on a survey of the Clinton area concerning the opinion of residents on the adult entertainment industry in Times Square. Over the past few years, the confusion about the Supreme Court's interpretation of what obscenity is has caused some concern among residents of the Times Square area because of the growth of the adult entertainment industry. We would be pleased to have your opinion on this important question.

1. You may know that most of the owners and operators of adult entertainment businesses claim the right to provide their services under the First Amendment to our Constitution, which guarantees freedom of speech and the press. Do you agree with this stand?

| YES | NO |
|-----|----|
| 1   | 2  |

1/

(SHOW CARD FOR Qs. 2 AND 3):

2. On the card is a list of some of the main activities which are considered "adult entertainment." Please look at the list and tell me one by one which activities you think are more visible in the community this past year; that is, since January 1976:

(If answer is "don't know" write 9)

| | Visible in community | | | |
|---|---|---|---|---|
| | More since 1976 | Less since 1976 | No change | |
| a. massage parlors | 2 | 1 | 3 | 2/ |
| b. films | 2 | 1 | 3 | 3/ |
| c. bookstores | 2 | 1 | 3 | 4/ |
| d. prostitutes approaching passersby | 2 | 1 | 3 | 5/ |
| e. signs outside places of adult entertainment | 2 | 1 | 3 | 6/ |
| f. topless bars | 2 | 1 | 3 | 7/ |
| g. topless and bottomless bars | 2 | 1 | 3 | 8/ |
| h. live sex theaters | 2 | 1 | 3 | 9/ |
| i. coin-operated entertainment (peep shows) | 2 | 1 | 3 | 10/ |

217

3. Look again at the list of activities related to the adult entertainment industry. Now tell me whether you personally object
to any or find any offensive. How do you regard them? Offensive or not? Please look at the scale on your card. If not
offensive, give me zero. If offensive, give me 1 through 9.

(If no answer
write 10)

|  | 0<br>Not Offensive | 1 - 9<br>Offensive |  |
|---|---|---|---|
| a. |  |  | 11-12/ |
| b. |  |  | 13-14/ |
| c. |  |  | 15-16/ |
| d. |  |  | 17-18/ |
| e. |  |  | 19-20/ |
| f. |  |  | 21-22/ |
| g. |  |  | 23-24/ |
| h. |  |  | 25-26/ |
| i. |  |  | 27-28/ |

218

(GIVE RESPONDENT EXTRA Q. 4 SHEET)

4. In this neighborhood, you may have noticed or met up with some
related activities of "adult entertainment", mainly as it occurs
in the streets. Consider the activities listed below. How do
you regard them? Offensive or not? If not, please state. If so,
make the least offensive one No. 1, and so on:

(If no answer,
write 10)

| | | 0<br>Not offensive | 1 - 9<br>Offensive | |
|---|---|---|---|---|
| a. | street "leafletting" by men advertising massage parlors | | | 29-30/ |
| b. | solicitation by prostitutes on streets | | | 31-32/ |
| c. | men standing outside massage parlors calling out availability of women inside | | | 33-34/ |
| d. | photos at entrances of massage parlors emphasizing female sexual anatomy | | | 35-36/ |
| e. | amplified sounds and flashing lights from adult film theaters and topless bars | | | 37-38/ |
| f. | noise connected with prostitution activities at night on streets, in parking or empty lots | | | 39-40/ |
| g. | cruising cars, looking for pickups | | | 41-42/ |
| h. | homosexual pickups in the area | | | 43-44/ |
| i. | transvestite solicitation on 10th Avenue | | | 45-46/ |

219

5. On the card are various types of sexual scenes which are included in current films. Look at the list. If one or more of these sexual scenes in a movie tells part of the story, do you think that this scene should be allowed?

(If no answer, write 9)

| | Definitely be allowed | Probably be allowed | Probably not be allowed | Definitely not be allowed | Don't Know | |
|---|---|---|---|---|---|---|
| a. scenes which show the sex organs of a man or a woman | 1 | 2 | 3 | 4 | 5 | 47/ |
| b. mouth-sex organ contact between a man and a woman | 1 | 2 | 3 | 4 | 5 | 48/ |
| c. a man and a woman having sexual intercourse | 1 | 2 | 3 | 4 | 5 | 49/ |
| d. sexual activities between people of the same sex | 1 | 2 | 3 | 4 | 5 | 50/ |
| e. anal intercourse | 1 | 2 | 3 | 4 | 5 | 51/ |
| f. sex activities which include whips, belts, or spankings | 1 | 2 | 3 | 4 | 5 | 52/ |

220

6. We have been talking about what people might or might not be allowed to see in films. Now tell me what your opinion is of public advertising of adult entertainment events, which everyone **can** see:

(If no answer, write 9)

| | Definitely be allowed | Probably be allowed | Probably not be allowed | Definitely not be allowed | D.K. | |
|---|---|---|---|---|---|---|
| a. photos outside massage parlors emphasizing female sexual parts | 1 | 2 | 3 | 4 | 5 | 53/ |
| b. photos outside theaters emphasizing male & female sexual **parts** | 1 | 2 | 3 | 4 | 5 | 54/ |
| c. **photos outside theaters showing** one person punishing another | 1 | 2 | 3 | 4 | 5 | 55/ |
| d. photos on magazine covers showing one person punishing another | 1 | 2 | 3 | 4 | 5 | 56/ |
| e. current newspaper advertisements of X-rated films | 1 | 2 | 3 | 4 | 5 | 57/ |
| f. men outside massage parlors handing out explicit leaflets about the women inside | 1 | 2 | 3 | 4 | 5 | 58/ |
| g. men outside massage parlors calling out about the availability of women inside | 1 | 2 | 3 | 4 | 5 | 59/ |
| h. prostitutes trying to make a contract on the street | 1 | 2 | 3 | 4 | 5 | 60/ |

221

7. If a movie theatre which generally shows G-rated films exhibits an X-rated one every once in a while, would you continue taking your family there for G-rated films?

(If no answer, write 9)

| YES | NO | D. K. |
|-----|----|----|
| 1 | 2 | 3 |

61/

8. Because of disagreement on the concept of obscenity, how would you feel if law enforcement officers harassed bookstores or film theatres by closing them down on the following grounds:

(If no answer, write 9)

| | AGREE | DISAGREE | |
|---|-------|----------|---|
| a. false advertising | 1 | 2 | 62/ |
| b. lack of air space | 1 | 2 | 63/ |
| c. non-compliance with fire code | 1 | 2 | 64/ |
| d. inadequate sanitary facilities | 1 | 2 | 65/ |
| e. unlicensed personnel performing service | 1 | 2 | 66/ |

9. Consider the Broadway show "O Calcutta" which advertises itself as a "sexual musical." It offers nudity and explicit sexual activity onstage. Times Square live sex shows offer the same entertainment. Which show do you think the City government would find reason to close? (If no answer, write 9)

| 1.<br>O Calcutta | 2.<br>Live Sex Show | 3.<br>Neither | 4.<br>Don't Know | |
|---|---|---|---|---|
| 1 | 2 | 3 | 4 | 67/ |

(IF RESPONSE IS 1 OR 2, THEN:)

10. Why do you think that?

_____

_____

_____  68/

223

(SHOW PHOTOGRAPHS OF MASSAGE PARLORS/THEATRE FRONTS):

11. Now I'd like you to look at these photographs of some adult
entertainment now offered in the Clinton neighborhood. Then
check off from the following list your reactions to the photos:

| (INTERVIEW ACROSS)<br>(If no opinion, write 3<br>If no answer, write 9) | 1.<br>Live Sex Theatre<br>'Show World"<br>Agree/Disagree | | 2.<br>Film:"Intimate<br>Teenagers"<br>Agree/Disagree | | 3.<br>Massage<br>Parlor<br>Agree/Disagree | |
|---|---|---|---|---|---|---|
| a. this place looks like a fire trap | 1 | 2 | 1 | 2 | 1 | 2 |
| b. this business brings jobs into the neighborhood | 1 | 2 | 1 | 2 | 1 | 2 |
| c. it brings more traffic into an area already congested | 1 | 2 | 1 | 2 | 1 | 2 |
| d. it brings venereal disease into the area | 1 | 2 | 1 | 2 | 1 | 2 |
| e. this place has a right to carry on business here | 1 | 2 | 1 | 2 | 1 | 2 |
| f. this place affects real estate values in the immediate area | 1 | 2 | 1 | 2 | 1 | 2 |
| g. it attracts undesirable loiterers who interfere with everyday business of Clinton residents | 1 | 2 | 1 | 2 | 1 | 2 |
| h. people want this service or it would not be there | 1 | 2 | 1 | 2 | 1 | 2 |
| i. it brings more crime into the neighborhood | 1 | 2 | 1 | 2 | 1 | 2 |

(SHOW 9 MAGAZINE COVERS):

12. Would you look at these magazine covers, which repre-
sent some publications currently available on newsstands
in the Clinton and Times Square areas. Please indicate
whether or not you think they're o.k. to display on
newsstands:

(If no opinion, write 3
If no answer, write 9)

|  | YES | NO |  |
|---|---|---|---|
| a. Playboy | 1 | 2 | 28/ |
| b. Oui | 1 | 2 | 29/ |
| c. Penthouse | 1 | 2 | 30/ |
| d. Hustler | 1 | 2 | 31/ |
| e. Screw | 1 | 2 | 32/ |
| f. Pleasure | 1 | 2 | 33/ |
| g. Affair | 1 | 2 | 34/ |
| h. Playgirl | 1 | 2 | 35/ |
| i. Chic | 1 | 2 | 36/ |

225

(SHOW 6 ALBUM COVER PHOTOS):

13. Here are some rock n' roll record album covers,
designed to sell to a teenage market and found in the
Times Square area. Give your opinion of them.

(If no opinion, write 3
If no answer, write 9)

| | A O.K. for under 17 to buy this | | B O.K. for over 17 to buy this | | C the cover picture should be changed | |
|---|---|---|---|---|---|---|
| | Y | N | Y | N | Y | N |
| a. Honey | 1 | 2 | 1 | 2 | 1 | 2 |
| b. Jefferson Starship | 1 | 2 | 1 | 2 | 1 | 2 |
| c. Jump On It | 1 | 2 | 1 | 2 | 1 | 2 |
| d. Linda Ronstadt | 1 | 2 | 1 | 2 | 1 | 2 |
| e. Choice Cuts | 1 | 2 | 1 | 2 | 1 | 2 |
| f. Donna Summer | 1 | 2 | 1 | 2 | 1 | 2 |

226

16. How would you vote for the following proposals?

(If no opinion, write 3
If no answer, write 9)

| | YES | NO | |
|---|---|---|---|
| a. the present City Planning Commission proposals:<br>- forbidding location of adult entertainment within 500 feet of a residential district | 1 | 2 | 63/ |
| - restricting the number of adult establishments within each zoning area | 1 | 2 | 64/ |
| b. a zoning law which would place all adult entertainment businesses in only one, non-residential part of the city | 1 | 2 | 65/ |
| c. decriminalize prostitution ( make it not punishable under the criminal code) | 1 | 2 | 66/ |
| d. legalize all adult entertainment businesses | 1 | 2 | 67/ |

227

(CIRCLE NUMBER GIVEN BY RESPONDENT): (SHOW CARD FOR Q.17):

17. Look at this list involving adult materials or activities and tell

me what you think should be done in each case.

Just give me the number. You may have several numbers for one answer.

| | | | | | | | |
|---|---|---|---|---|---|---|---|
| a. street "leafletting" by men advertising massage parlors | 1 | 2 | 3 | 4 | 5 | 6 | 1-6/ |
| b. solicitation by prostitutes in streets | 1 | 2 | 3 | 4 | 5 | 6 | 7-12/ |
| c. men standing in front of massage parlors, calling out availability of women inside | 1 | 2 | 3 | 4 | 5 | 6 | 13-18/ |
| d. photos at entrances of massage parlors emphasizing female sexual anatomy | 1 | 2 | 3 | 4 | 5 | 6 | 19-24/ |
| e. amplified sounds and flashing lights from adult theatres and topless bars | 1 | 2 | 3 | 4 | 5 | 6 | 25-30/ |
| f. topless and bottomless live theaters | 1 | 2 | 3 | 4 | 5 | 6 | 31-36/ |
| g. noise connected with prostitution activities at night on streets and in parking or empty lots | 1 | 2 | 3 | 4 | 5 | 6 | 37-42/ |
| h. traffic flow of cars cruising the area looking for a pickup | 1 | 2 | 3 | 4 | 5 | 6 | 43-48/ |
| i. homosexual pickups in the area | 1 | 2 | 3 | 4 | 5 | 6 | 49-54/ |
| j. transvestite solicitation up and down 10th Avenue | 1 | 2 | 3 | 4 | 5 | 6 | 55-60/ |

1. Pass legislation to keep off street
2. Nothing
3. Citizen action: organize and demonstrate
4. Police should enforce existing laws
5. Pass legislation totally forbidding this
6. Organize local businessmen to put
   pressure on lawmakers about this

228

(IF "NO", THEN Q. 19)

'8. Do you know who these people are? If you do, you know they
are active Clinton leaders who have taken a public position on
the question of adult material businesses in Times Square and on
prostitution. Please mark down what kind of a job you think they
are doing regarding adult businesses and activities:

|  |  | GOOD | FAIR | POOR | D.K. |  |  |
|---|---|---|---|---|---|---|---|
| (If no answer, write 9) | a. Democratic District Party leaders: Jas. R. McManus Mary d'Elia | 1 | 2 | 3 | 4 | | 1/ |
| | b. Republican District Party leaders: John Doyle, Ann Sanaga | 1 | 2 | 3 | 4 | | 2/ |
| | c. Protestant Church leaders: Rev. Dale Hanson, S. Luke's, W. 46th St. | 1 | 2 | 3 | 4 | | 3/ |
| | d. Roman Catholic Church leaders: Rev. Robert Rappelyea, Holy Cross Church, W. 42nd St. | 1 | 2 | 3 | 4 | | 4/ |
| | e. Kenneth P. Norwick, lawyer, American Civil Liberties Union | 1 | 2 | 3 | 4 | | 5/ |
| | f. Former Head, Commt'y. Bd. No. 4 Mr. Aston Glaves | 1 | 2 | 3 | 4 | | 6/ |
| | g. Head, Clinton Planning Council, Mr. Jas. Naun | 1 | 2 | 3 | 4 | | 7/ |
| | h. Mr. A.M. Rosenthal, Editor, The New York TIMES | 1 | 2 | 3 | 4 | | 8/ |
| | i. Mr. M.J. O'Neill, Editor, DAILY NEWS | 1 | 2 | 3 | 4 | | 9/ |

229

(SHOW CARD FOR Q. 19:)

19. Would you check off from the list below what you think are the three most serious problems related to the adult entertainment industry in the Clinton community. Make the most serious No. 1:

(Write in 3 answers in rank order: )

_____

_____

_____

| | | 10 -<br>12/ |
|---|---|---|
| 0 | prostitution on 8th and 10th Avenues | |
| 1 | the attention it is getting uses up resources better directed to dealing with better housing, street crime, drug abuse | |
| 2 | spread of sex businesses to the 50's | |
| 3 | harassment on street from sex businesses | |
| 4 | deterioration of neighborhood | |
| 5 | politicians use this community's concern over the problem for their own political purposes | |
| 6 | encourages the idea that in sexual behavior, anything men and women do to each other is o.k. | |
| 7 | effect on children growing up in area | |
| 8 | the public statements made by community leaders bring about political solutions which will probably be declared unconstitutional by the courts | |
| 9 | the support of organized crime for sex businesses | |

230

20. Now I would like to ask you some background questions. First, how long have you lived in Clinton? _____ 13-14/

21. How old are you? _____ 15-16/

22. How many children under 17 live in this household? _____ 17/

23. Are you:

| | | 18/ |
|---|---|---|
| 1 | Single | |
| 2 | Married | |
| 3 | Divorced | |
| 4 | Separated | |
| 5 | Widowed | |

24. What is your occupation?

| | | | | 19/ |
|---|---|---|---|---|
| 1 | Civil Service | 7 | Performing/ Fine Arts | |
| 2 | Domestic | | | |
| 3 | Homemaker | 8 | Professional | |
| 4 | Manual | 9 | Self-employed | |
| 5 | Managerial | 10 | Student | |
| 6 | Office Worker | 11 | Other | |

25. What was the last grade that you completed in school?

| | | | | | | | | | 20-21/ |
|---|---|---|---|---|---|---|---|---|---|
| Elementary school | 1 | 2 | 3 | 4 | 5 | 6 | 7 | 8 | |
| High school | 9 | 10 | 11 | 12 | | | | | |
| Vocational school | 21 | 22 | 23 | 24 | | | | | |
| College | 13 | 14 | 15 | 16 | | | | | |
| Postgraduate work | 17 | 18 | 19 | 20 | | | | | |

(SHOW CARD FOR Q. 26:)

26. In which of these income groups was your total family income for 1976? That would be before taxes. Just give me the letter:

| | | | 22/ |
|---|---|---|---|
| 1 | a. | below $2,000 | |
| 2 | b. | $2,000 - 4,999 | |
| 3 | c. | $5,000 - 7,999 | |
| 4 | d. | $8,000 - 11,999 | |
| 5 | e. | $12,000 - 14,999 | |
| 6 | f. | $15,000 - 19,999 | |
| 7 | g. | $20,000 - | |

(INTERVIEWER RECORD FROM OBSERVATION):

27.

| | M | F | 23/ |
|---|---|---|---|
| Sex | 1 | 2 | |

28.

| Race | 1 | White | 24/ |
|---|---|---|---|
| | 2 | Black | |
| | 3 | Hispanic | |
| | 4 | Oriental | |
| | 5 | Other | |

Time interview ended _____ A.M. _____ P.M.

231

INDEX

## A STANDARD FOR MILLER

adult entertainment industry, 23
  crime. See crime
  fire hazards, 54, 102, 105, 106, 117,
  118, 129, 137-38, 140
  increase in traffic, 138, 140
  lack of air space, 101, 102, 104, 105
  lack of sanitary conditions, 102, 105,
  107
  loiterers, 39, 58, 87, 124, 130
  neighborhood jobs, 87, 117, 119-20
  real estate values, 56, 58, 122, 124,
  125, 138, 185
  unlicensed personnel, 102, 108, 109
  See also specific topics

advertising, 67, 69-70, 90, 147, 157
  false advertsing, 101, 102, 103, 105

Affair, 80

American Civil Liberties Union, 4

American Mini-Theatre Inc.; Young v.,
  3-4, 6

anti-pornography crusades, 10-12
  "Spotlight on Smut" rally, 49

arrest statistics, 59, 60, 61

Baumgartner, Sidney, 49

Beame, Mayor Abraham, 16, 49
  closing of "Show World,", 46, 47, 89

bookstores: offensiveness rating, 41

bottomless bars, 65
  offensiveness rating, 51

Brennan, Justice William, 5-6

Burger, Chief Justice Warren, 3

freedom of speech and the press. <u>See</u>
First Amendment rights

Greitzer, Carol 22

Gusfield, J.R., 11-12, 200

Harlan, Justice John, 13

Holy Cross Catholic Church, 49, 195

homosexual prostitution, 162, 165

<u>Hustler</u>, 80

"intimate Teenagers," 46, 55, 118, 119,
121, 123, 126, 128

<u>Jacksonville; Erznoznik v.</u>, 186

<u>Jacobellis v. Ohio</u>, 13-14

John Jay College of Criminal Justice, 28

Kirkpatrick, R. George, 10-11, 12, 41, 126

live sex shows
offensiveness rating, 42, 53
theatrical production compared,
143-47

magazines, 36, 70-80, 90

Manhattan Plaza Project, 199

massage parlors, 47, 49
crime, 164
offensivness rating, 48
"Pillow Talk," 47, 51-52, 66, 88-89

real estate values, 122
venereal disease, 54, 164

Midtown Citizens' Committee, 49

Mid-Town Law Enforcement Project, 49,
 52

<u>Miller v. California</u>, 2, 3, 4, 9, 13, 15, 96

"Minnesota Strip," 49

movies, 62, 64. <u>See also</u> "Intimate Teenagers"

narcotics:  arrest statistics, 60

National Coalition Against Censorship, 4

New York City Planning Commission, 7, 21,
 36, 94, 131, 159, 171-72

nuisance, 7-9, 155, 192-93
 definition, 23-25
 <u>per accidens</u>, 24
 <u>per se</u>, 24-25
 private, 8, 25
 public, 7, 8, 25

Nuisance Abatement Law, 9, 16-18

"O Calcutta," 143-47, 149, 151-56

obscenity:
 arrest statistics, 60
 definition, 22

<u>Ohio; Jacobellis v.</u>, 13-14

<u>Oui</u>, 70, 80

Papert, Fred, 66

red light districts, 159

Remeny; People v., 93

Rendelman, D., 9

Report on Pornography and Obscenity, 61

Rizzo, Mayor Frank L., 15

Roth v. United States, 2, 3

sado-masochism: advertising, 70, 90

Screw, 70, 80, 90

sex crimes: arest statistics, 60, 61

sex entertainment industry. See adult entertainment industry

"Show World," 46, 67, 89, 118, 119, 121, 123

Slaton; Paris Adult Theatre I v., 3, 5-6

Smelser, N.J., 12

Smith v. United States, 4, 5, 6

"Spotlight on Smut" rally, 49

Statistical Package for Social Sciences (SPSS-G), 28

Stevens, Justice John, 4, 5

temperance movement, 11-12